WAY OF INSIGHT

A Guide to Meditation

QUYEN NGO

Way of Insight:
A Guide to Meditation
By Quyen Ngo

Published by Quyen Ngo

All rights reserved. No part of this book may be reproduced or transmitted in any form or by any means, electronic or mechanical, including photocopying, recording or by any information storage and retrieval system, without written permission from the author.

Copyright © 2020 by Quyen Ngo First Edition, 2020
Cover design by Dewi Hong

Print ISBN: 978-0-6485171-1-5

To Mom and Dad

I don't envision a single thing that, when developed and cultivated, leads to such great benefit as the mind. The mind, when developed and cultivated, leads to great benefit.
　　　　　　　　　　　　　　　　　　　　　—The Buddha[1]

Table of Contents

Title i
Copyright ii
Dedication iii
Epigraph iv
About the author vii
Acknowledgments ix

Introduction 1

Chapter 1 The Benefits of Meditation 9
1.1 Contentment Here Now 9
1.2 Physical and Psychological Benefits of Meditation 9
1.3 Meditation for Transformation 12
1.4 Meditation for Psychotherapy 14
1.5 The Spiritual Benefit of Meditation 17
1.6 Being in the Moment 21

Chapter 2 The Preparation 25
2.1 Postures in Meditation 25
2.2 The Preliminary Practice 31

Chapter 3 *Metta* (Loving-Kindness) Meditation 35

Chapter 4 Mindfulness of Breathing (*Anapanasati*) Meditation 43
4.1 Stage 1: Mindfulness with Labeling 45

4.2 Stage 2: Mindfulness with Counting 48

4.3 Stage 3: Long or Short 50

4.4 Stage 4: Beginning, Middle, or End 50

4.5 Stage 5: Full, Sustained Attention on the Breath 51

4.6 Concentration *(Samatha)* Walking Meditation 53

4.7 The Sound of Silence Meditation 55

Chapter 5 *Nimitta* (Visions) 59

Chapter 6 The Hindrances: Enemies of Meditation 63

Chapter 7 Insight *(Vipassana)* Meditation 71
7.1 *Vedanna* (Sensation) Insight Meditation 75

7.2 *Citta* (Mental objects) Insight Meditation 77

7.3 Insight *(Vipassana)* Walking Meditation 78

Chapter 8 The Role of Wise Attention 83

Chapter 9 Dangers in Meditation 87

Chapter 10 Putting It All Together 93

Glossary 107
Bibliography 109
Footnotes and References 111

About the author

Quyen Ngo is a Buddhist studies scholar and a keen meditator.

He has been practicing meditation since 1992 and has participated in numerous meditation retreats in the UK, New Zealand, Australia, and Myanmar.

He completed a master's degree in Buddhist Studies with a UK-based university in 2007, and since then he has published a number of books and articles on meditation and Buddhism.

Having invested almost three decades in meditation and Buddhist studies, Quyen enjoys sharing his knowledge on topics that are close to his heart.

Acknowledgments

I would like to express my sincere gratitude to the following people:

Sayadaw Venerable Eikdi Bala, my first meditation teacher in Myanmar. My sincere gratitude for his generous teaching, which gave rise to the insights detailed in my book, *Diary of a Meditator*.

Sayadaw Venerable Baddanta Dhammapati, my second meditation teacher in Myanmar. Thank you for months of tutelage and care in your forest meditation center.

I remain greatly indebted to Venerable Jharnote Kansa and his family, who have supported me in my all meditation retreats in Myanmar.

I am grateful to all my teachers in the past and present for your sharing of knowledge and wisdom.

Gratitude to my family for their love and support in all my endeavors.

Special thanks to Dewi Hong for creating the beautiful cover for this book.

Introduction

Whatever an enemy might do to an enemy...
the ill-directed mind can do to you even worse.
Whatever a mother, father, or other kinsman might do for
you, the well-directed mind can do for you even better.
—The Buddha[2]

We all want contentment in our lives, yet only a few of us can honestly say that we are truly content under most circumstances. This is because most of the time we are running in the opposite direction! Instead of enjoying living in the present moment, our minds are forever chasing something else that might make us even happier: "When I get this..." "Once I obtain that..." "Once I win the lottery..." Happiness, then, is an illusion that is rarely fulfilled. Even when we get what we want, we are still not content, because the mind has already moved on to other desires. Our never-ending tasks create an undercurrent of something lacking or unsatisfactory in our lives. Similarly, we might suffer anxiety over something that might never materialize. And all of this comes from unrealistic expectations — illusions we created from our own wandering mind.

This has been humanity's dilemma for centuries. Fortunately, there were people bold enough to dedicate their lives to tackling this quandary. Over 2,500 years ago, the Buddha realized the way to attain serenity wasn't to fulfill every one of our desires, but rather to look into our own mind to assess whether those desires were justified, or were they, in fact, the source of our suffering. The insight he uncovered was one of letting go rather than accumulation. He thus liberated his own mind from mental bondage. And although his teaching was completely contrary to most people's way of thinking, there were those wise enough to listen, and they too were liberated.

You could say what the Buddha discovered and taught was the art of contentment and liberation. As with any art, it requires training and effort. Here, the training involves observing the mind. Only through observing it can you understand that the mind's unrealistic tendencies invariably lead to disappointment. The insights you obtain will be from your own verifiable experience, so you do not have to take anyone's word for it. This is crucial. Only *you* can change yourself — nobody else can.

This book on the art of contentment presents you with a set of skills designed for you to master your own mind and to obtain insights that will bring equanimity wherever you are and whatever situation you find yourself in. It will help you to realize contentment *here* and *now*. You don't have to be anything or go anywhere — you've already got all the tools you need to succeed. You just need the craft to shape your mind, and this is what the art is all about.

Your mind is like a garden; landscape and cultivate it so you can enjoy its beauty. Left untended, it will be filled with weeds.

Over these pages, I will share with you the wisdom of the sages: how to observe the mind to obtain insights. Of course, you cannot observe the mind without the power of concentration, so that forms the foundation of our training.

I will show you how you can recognize harmful and beneficial states of mind, how to cultivate positive mental states, and how to weed out the negative ones. You will learn how to calm your mind to become concentrated. When the mind is concentrated, insights will naturally arise.

Also, when your mind is concentrated, every aspect of your life will be better. Your memory will improve, your work will be more productive, your interactions more meaningful, and your senses heightened. Even the trees and the sky will appear more vivid and colorful. The clarity you'd get with a concentrated mind will make your previous mental state seem dull and drowsy. This is because a concentrated mind is more engaged in the present moment.

The practice will also help you to develop compassion, and the heightened empathy will help you to become more tolerant and less stressed. This in turn fuels concentration.

With continued insight practice, you will start to uproot the negative tendencies (such as phobias, fears, insecurities, and anxieties) as they are now seen under new perspectives. You will have a better understanding of yourself, others, the natural world we live in, and the interconnectedness of all things.

The book begins with the benefits of meditation, then moves on to techniques in how to practice concentration and insight, and finally how to select and combine techniques in a program suitable for your needs, similar to the way you would employ certain exercises to develop strength or stamina that is unique for your sport. Therefore, it is important to read the final chapter before you begin to practice.

It is important that you adhere strictly to the instructions given. Please do not mix with what you have been doing or what you have read elsewhere. This method is structured to work exactly as prescribed below. You will not get the results as intended if you mix with other techniques. So forget all that you have known and empty your mind before you begin this practice.

The techniques outlined in this book I drew from the teachings of my two renowned Burmese masters in the Theravada tradition, Sayadaw Venerable Eikdi Bala[3] and Venerable Baddanta Dhammapati. I am very grateful for their patient guidance and for allowing me to share their knowledge with others. Thus, you can now benefit from their teaching in the comfort of your own home without having to ward off pesky mosquitoes in the sweltering forests of Myanmar.

After months of guidance with daily interviews on the art of mindfulness and concentration, I distilled the most salient points to share with you. I hope this teaching will be a big eye-opener for you, the reader, as it was for me.

You might ask: what makes this book any different to hundreds out there on mindfulness meditation? In fact, even the word "mindfulness" is such a cliché now. Well, from my own experience, I was embarrassed to admit I had many years of experience in meditation before I met my teachers. They made me feel like I knew *nothing* at all! Mindfulness of breathing was so profoundly subtle that after months of all-day meditation, I still had so many questions to ask. Bearing this in mind, I have made the instructions as detailed as possible to the point of repeating myself in places. I suggest you read the instructions repeatedly, because each time you read, a certain concept may become clearer after you have had some practice. The depth, scope, and the way you employ the techniques is what makes this book different to others on the subject, as was reflected in my own experience when I met my teachers. I am hoping it will have the same effect for you.

After some experimentation, I discovered my own systematic approach in training that was useful to structure my progress in a step-by-step manner such that I was able to quickly "scale" up or down the techniques I employ, depending on the condition of my mind during the practice. It also helped me to know exactly the stages of my training and to monitor progress. I called it Systematic Progressing, which I present in the final chapter of this book. If you prefer to work in structure and to be able to gauge of the stages of your concentration, you may find this useful; if not, leave it aside.

This book is all about practice and getting results. As such, despite my Buddhist scholarly background, I have deliberately left out much discussion on Buddhist philosophy, of which you'll find plenty elsewhere. You do not need to know this to practice. Here, the emphasis is practice, practice, and practice. In fact, it is detrimental to your practice if I fill your mind with much more than bare instructions — doing so would only incite your wandering mind! The aim is for you to focus only on your meditation object and nothing else. When you've developed sufficient concentration, you will realize the insights for yourself. No descriptions from anyone else suffice.

When I came to my masters for training, one of the first things they said to me was that I needed to forget what I learned before. This was easier said than done, especially when you've been educated to question and analyze everything. I found my academic background only served as an obstacle in my training. So, if you're a complete beginner, consider yourself lucky. Otherwise, you may have a lot of unlearning to do.

Please make sure you understand the techniques clearly before you practice, and then just do it. Don't think of anything else. The more you think, the less concentrated you get.

I wish you success and enjoyment in developing your mind. May you awaken to new insights.

Quyen Ngo, 2020

https://www.wayofinsight.com

Email: qngo@wayofinsight.com

Chapter 1
The Benefits of Meditation

1.1 Contentment Here Now

To truly live and experience, we have to abide in the present moment. It is in this very brief and transient moment that we experience the world, not in the past or the future. Yet most of the time our mind dwells in the past or the future.[4] This preoccupation of the mind means we only truly live some of the time — when we are fully immersed in what we do.

Thinking about the past brings anger, regret, and remorse. Thinking about the future makes us anxious, worried, and fearful. Meditation trains the mind to abide in the present moment. When you focus on the present, thoughts about the past and future disappear, just as light chases away darkness.

As your meditation progresses, you will enjoy living in the moment, taking delight in the child-like mind amid the simplest activity. You will have better concentration, power of recall, make better decisions, and be freer from worries.

1.2 Physical and Psychological Benefits of Meditation

Research shows that meditation for as little as ten minutes a day can make a dramatic difference to one's physical and mental health.[5] Benefits from meditation come after just a few weeks of practice.

In *The Physical and Psychological Effects of Meditation* (1997), Michael Murphy and Steven Donovan consolidated numerous studies from the past few decades of works carried out by researchers on the effects of meditation. They include:[6]

- Lower heart rate
- Change in blood flow (for example, empathy is related to the flushing of particular body parts such as the face and chest)
- Lower blood pressure
- Help with cardiovascular diseases such as angina and hypercholesterolemia
- Lessened stress
- Heightened perceptual awareness
- Improved reaction time and motor skill (due to increased alertness)
- Improved concentration and attention (less likely to be distracted)
- Improved memory
- Increased empathy (a person becomes kinder)
- More developed equanimity and detachment
- Increased experience of rapture and bliss
- More vivid and more archetypal dreams, a higher dream recall rate
- Experiences bordering on extrasensory or parapsychological perception
- Altered body image and ego boundaries

- Increased energy and excitement after meditation and clearer visual perception and greater awareness of bodily processes.

Jon Kabat-Zinn of the University of Massachusetts Medical Center conducted a successful eight-week Mindfulness-Based Stress Reduction (MBSR) program, using meditation to treat stress in patients suffering from a wide range of conditions. The program enjoyed success to the extent that it was later offered to medical students and hospital staff.[7]

In 1982, Kabat-Zinn showed mindfulness meditation was an effective way to control pain (Silva, 1990), because meditators were able to "decouple" the physical sensation from the psychological elaboration. For most people, physical pain is usually accompanied by psychological pain in the form of grief, restlessness, and worry. The Buddha said it was like being shot with two arrows. The first arrow is the physical pain, and the psychological pain is like the second arrow. A wise person, however, by remaining equanimous, only suffers the pain of the first arrow, the physical pain, and not psychological pain of grief or worry, the second arrow.

Considering the above benefits, it is no wonder that meditation has been used in psychotherapy to help patients develop self-esteem, enhance relationships, and in treating conditions such as depression, anxiety, chronic pain, and childhood distress.

1.3 Meditation for Transformation

Meditation is for personal transformation. "In all types of mysticism and in many spiritual traditions, meditation is the path to a pure and empowered mind," says Ajahn Brahmavamso. "The experience of this pure mind, released from the world, is incredibly blissful."[8]

"The benefits of meditation are two-fold," says Ajahn Brahmali, a Buddhist monk of over eleven years standing and another resident of the Bodhinyana Buddhist Monastery.[9] "The 'ordinary' benefit of meditation, like getting rid of depression, anxiety, and stress [allows you to] feel more peaceful, more relaxed, more at ease," he says, "because you feel more peaceful, more relaxed, you become more efficient in your work and you become a more pleasant person to be around. So you become more socially adept. All of these things go together."

In ordinary life, most of us are generally unaware of our negative attributes. As a result, we make mistakes and do unintended harm to others and ourselves by making the wrong decisions and saying the wrong things. Being mindful of our traits, through careful observation (meditation), allows us to "know ourselves." This in turn helps us to take responsibility for our actions as we become more aware of our previous blind spots. Therefore, we can make wiser decisions and enjoy more amicable relationships.

"Apart from the worldly side, there is [also] the spiritual side of meditation, [which can be] divided into two parts. One is the feeling of meditation — when you experience joy, peace, happiness, and tranquility. And the other aspect is the insight aspect — where you come to understand the mind and the body. You understand what you're truly like; you understand the world around you, basically," says Ajahn Brahmali. "[Hence,] you become wiser and you have less suffering. That's what wisdom is all about. You have less suffering and you can help other people."

Meditation increases concentration, awareness, tranquility, and it sharpens our ability to think. Simultaneously, it reduces tension, fear, restlessness, and worry.

"The general effects of meditation are a gradual increase in calm and awareness. A person becomes more patient, better able to deal with the ups and downs of life, clearer-headed and more energetic," says Dr. Peter Harvey, a professor of Buddhist Studies and meditation teacher. "He becomes both more open in his dealings with others, and more self-confident and able to stand his own ground."[10]

Meditation is also relaxing and enjoyable; the Buddha referred to it as "pleasant abiding." Ajahn Brahmavamso, the abbot of the Bodhinyana Buddhist Monastery in Western Australia, who described himself as a "meditation junkie," says it is "a bliss better than sex."[11]

I found meditation can certainly be "addictive," and it gives you a "clean" high. Sometimes all you want to do is sit. And you could sit for hours and not feeling tired or achy afterward. But before you get to that stage, there is quite a bit of slogging do to as you battle with the untrained mind.

1.4 Meditation for Psychotherapy

In 2009, I interviewed Dr. Christopher Walsh, a consultant psychiatrist for Turning Point Alcohol and Drug Centre in Melbourne, Australia, who prescribed meditation as part of the treatment for his patients. This was what he had to say:[12]

> *I was doing it [meditation] for a long, long time before I decided to formally introduce it to patients. Firstly, I felt it was very helpful in my own life: it helped me to be more flexible, to cope with stress, to remain compassionate and not be reactive to things in a bad way. So I could stay calm and help people through crisis. So I found that the first application of meditation to my work was actually just to create a healing space for patients by me meditating, not by teaching them to meditate. That's probably the most important application.*
>
> *You'd find that when you're creating a meditation space, even without saying anything about it, you'd find your patients becoming a bit more flexible and more capable of responding in a good way to the challenges around them. I think we've all had our experiences too, when we're in the presence of meditation masters, that our minds become open. So we can all create that opening, that meditation space.*

Dr. Walsh also had a private practice in North Carlton, Victoria. He explained how he came to use meditation in practice:

> *When I went into private practice, I wasn't dealing with people who were quite so sick.*

> *[But] when I was in public-sector psychiatry, I was dealing with people who were psychotic, and they weren't really up to doing the kind of meditation practices that I had learned. And in fact, that could in some ways make them worse. So I didn't teach them that.*
>
> *But when I went into private practice, I was dealing with a different population of people who were suffering from depression and anxiety. And I started to experiment with it.'*
>
> *And then a number of years later, a lot of researches started to appear showing the value of mindfulness meditation, and so I started to be more formally teaching it, at that point, once I had the confidence of having the research and the professional support, rather than being something that was a bit on the outside.*

Dr. Walsh has researched and published papers on mindfulness meditation in psychotherapy. He said he suspected some psychiatrists had been incorporating meditation into psychotherapy very quietly for decades, but only in the last decade had it become more overt. He thought meditation could be adapted to benefit a wide range of mental conditions besides depression.

> *There is certainly good proof for it [meditation] being helpful in preventing relapse in people with chronic relapses in depression. There's good research for that. I think it's applicable in a whole lot of range of conditions, but it needs to be approached in different ways.*
>
> *People who have problems with personality*

disorders or drug addictions or serious psychotic illnesses like schizophrenia — first you need to get them reasonably stable, and then you can teach them meditation techniques, but often in an adapted way.

Say you might start with what we might call "Meditation In Action" — merely bringing mindfulness to day-to-day activities like brushing your teeth, washing the dishes, or driving the car. In that way, it doesn't bring up too many difficult feelings. Normal meditation can bring up a lot of problems like agitation, boredom, grief, and that can overwhelm some people.

What I'm saying is that you just have to tailor it.

Dr. Walsh took a step-by-step approach in introducing meditation to his patients and encouraged them to apply it in everyday situations:

Generally, I'd do some exercises in the therapy room. Explain to them what the technique is and actually do the meditation with them for a little while and ask them about their experience afterward, and clarify any simple misunderstandings. And then to encourage them to experiment with it in their lives, and then gradually introduce [to] them Mindfulness in Action practices and see which they go with: whether they go with Mindfulness in Action or sitting meditation or both. Sometimes that experience is enough for them to realize that they are more than their thoughts, which is a good start.

> *Sometimes, people just find they get so much agitation that I would send them along to yoga classes or some kind of movement work, which can be very helpful as well, and also it may get them ready for meditation practice further down the track.*

Dr. Walsh admitted it was hard to establish a success rate, because meditation was part of the general therapy, so it was not easy to work out what was causing the success. However, he noticed that people who had developed a regular sitting practice had progressed quite a bit faster in their therapy than those who hadn't. "I have seen people plodding along and not doing very well and then starting to meditate and going ahead much faster once they started to meditate, so that I guess is pretty good evidence [of the beneficial effects of meditation]," he added.

Dr. Walsh said most people started to notice some benefits after a couple of weeks, if they were meditating every day, for about twenty minutes or more. "Then they start to notice some things: for a start, they notice they are not identifying with their thoughts so much, and they often find that they are a bit calmer during the day. Later on, they start to notice some more significant things, like they become more flexible and dealing with more difficult situations."

1.5 The Spiritual Benefit of Meditation

> *"Luminous, monks, is the mind. And it is defiled by incoming defilements."*[13]

According to Early Buddhism, the nature of the

mind, at the deepest level, is naturally pure and "brightly shining." This latent, dynamic, ground-state continuum consciousness, imbued with loving-kindness and wisdom called the *bhavanga-citta* in Pali, flows on like a smooth, flowing river.

During waking moments, there is very rapid alternation between this pure unconscious mind and the conscious states that perceive sensory and mental objects. When we react to objects without clear understanding, it gives rise to craving and aversion, forming the "defilements" that obscure the pure mind.

Obscurations of the mind distort the true perception of things, just as wearing tinted glasses would change the colors of the surroundings. They arise from our dualistic tendencies toward the objects we sense. That is, we tend to judge things as good or bad, desirable or undesirable. The more we do this, the more defilement we add onto the pure mind. And the more the defilements, the less the wisdom, and thus more associated suffering. And since defilements arise from unwholesome roots, they can only yield unwholesome fruits.

However, although the defilements stain the pure mind, they cannot change its inherently pure nature, because they come from extraneous unwholesome roots of delusion, greed, and aversion. They are not inherently part of the "pure" mind. Thus, under all the defilements and obscurations lies the stainless and intrinsically radiant mind that has potential for enlightenment. This concept became known as the Buddha-nature.

Ajahn Chah said:

In truth, there is nothing really wrong with it.

It is intrinsically pure. Within itself it's already peaceful. That the mind is not peaceful these days is because it follows moods. The real mind doesn't have anything to it; it is simply (an aspect of) Nature. It becomes peaceful or agitated because moods deceive it. The untrained mind is stupid. Sense impressions come and trick it into happiness, suffering, gladness, and sorrow, but the mind's true nature is none of those things. That gladness or sadness is not the mind, but only a mood coming to deceive us. The untrained mind gets lost and follows these things; it forgets itself. Then we think that it is we who are upset or at ease or whatever.

But really this mind of ours is already unmoving and peaceful...really peaceful! Just like a leaf, which is still as long as no wind blows. If a wind comes up, the leaf flutters. The fluttering is due to the wind — the "fluttering" is due to those sense impressions; the mind follows them. If it doesn't follow them, it doesn't "flutter." If we know fully the true nature of sense impressions, we will be unmoved.

Our practice is simply to see the Original Mind. So we must train the mind to know those sense impressions and not get lost in them. To make it peaceful. Just this is the aim of all this difficult practice we put ourselves through.[14]

That the radiant mind could be seen as Buddha-nature inherent in all beings expresses a very positive view and forms a basis for development and realization.

This is the reason why Buddhism has respect for all forms of life, since even the smallest sentient being has Buddha-nature and is capable of attaining enlightenment. For the same reason, Buddhism does not condemn anyone as inherently evil, even though a person might have committed atrocious deeds and had a very defiled mind. However, at the deepest level, his or her mind is still intrinsically pure and has the capacity to reveal its brightly shining nature by removing the defilements — through mental cultivation, as related by this famous story in the Buddhist sutta: [15]

At the time of the Buddha, there was a famous ruthless serial killer known as Angulimala because he used to wear a garland (*mala*) of the victims' fingers (*anguli*) around his neck. One day, the Buddha set out on the road where this killer was staying. Seeing this, villagers tried to dissuade him from taking that route, telling him that a feared killer was residing there. The Buddha, however, walked on in silence.

The killer, seeing Buddha from afar, thought, *Isn't it amazing! Isn't it astounding! Groups of ten, twenty, thirty, and forty men have gone along this road, and even they have fallen into my hands, and yet now this contemplative comes attacking, as it were, alone and without a companion. Why don't I kill him?*

So, taking up weapons, Angulimala followed the Buddha. However, by way of the Buddha's psychic power, no matter how fast Angulimala was running, he could not catch up to the Buddha who was walking at normal pace. So he thought, *Isn't it amazing that I chased and seized even a swift horse, elephant, and chariot, and yet I can't catch up to this monk walking at normal pace, even though I'm running with all my might!* So he stopped and called out, "Stop! Monk, stop!"

"I *have* stopped, Angulimala. *You* stop!" the Buddha replied.

Greatly puzzled, but sensing there was wisdom in that phrase, Angulimala asked, "Why did you say you have stopped when you were still walking, and why did you tell me to stop when I've already stopped?"

The Buddha explained he had "stopped" acts of violence, whilst Angulimala hadn't.

The impressed Angulimala suddenly came to his senses and became the Buddha's disciple. And under the Buddha's guidance, Angulimala practiced meditation steadfastly until he became enlightened. Despite the atrocious crimes he committed, Angulimala could still redeem himself through mental cultivation. I guess that makes the job seem much easier for the rest of us who are not serial killers.

1.6 Being in the Moment

"Being in the moment" has become a cliché since Zen was introduced to the West in the 1950s and 1960s. It has a broad spectrum of meaning these days, ranging from enjoying what one does, to being mindful of what one does, to being so totally absorbed in what one does that one is oblivious of the time, place, and environment. It is the latter case that gives rise to an exquisite joy that makes activities, be they work or play, highly addictive.

A musician can be so engrossed in playing an instrument he only hears the music but is unaware of the physical sensations of playing the instrument. A motorcyclist feels so at one with his machine travelling at a high speed that even the bike doesn't seem to exist, only the twists and turns of the road. A surfer feels part of the wave, in perfect harmony with nature's force. In all these cases, and more, people speak of getting into a spiritual stage where they become at one with what they do; in other words, they are living "in the moment."

Have you ever wondered why nature appeared much more captivating as a child? Looking back on my childhood, one of the most prominent features was that nature appeared more vivid and striking compared with how I later viewed things. I saw so much beauty in the texture and color of a lump of clay, veiny patterns on a leaf were intriguingly sophisticated and elaborate, I saw fauna and flora on a patch of grass, the patterns and texture of the bark on a tree were perplexedly intricate, and even the pores on bricks appeared mesmerizing. Those were the things I sorely missed turning into adulthood — until I went on my first meditation retreat when I could again dip into the same experience.

After a few days of practicing *anapanasati* (mindfulness of breathing), I observed much more beauty and radiance in the world around me. Flowers were brighter and more colorful. I noticed their petals and stamens were perfectly crafted and symmetrical, grass and trees appeared greener, skies bluer, sunrises and sunsets were more dramatic and stunning. It was like a transition from watching a small analogue television to a large 3D high-definition screen. Everything was more vivid, colorful, and in greater detail.

One day, after a good session of *samadhi* (concentration), I looked at an anthill next to some dead wood and saw a miniature world of creatures going about their daily life — a whole society of crawling, flying, and jumping insects amongst the variety of weeds on a patch of grass. What at first glance appeared like waste and chaos were, in fact, orderly, designed, and purposeful. Everything in that miniature world had a part to play in the whole. A heap of rubbish was, in fact, a universe of its own! And then wherever I looked, there was a complexity of life in the natural world. And everything was just perfect the way it was, such that if even a single thing were to change, it would affect the whole complex network. Right there and then, I was transported back into my childhood.

It dawned on me that this had a direct connection with the mystical spiritual experience people got when they became totally absorbed in something. The common denominator in all this was concentration and mindfulness.

Lack of concentration and mindfulness, usually because of mental dullness and distracting thoughts, pollute (or interfere with) our perception, similar to the way bad weather interferes with TV reception, resulting in fuzzy pictures. Concentration and mindfulness remove the filters that normally color our perception, allowing us to see things more clearly and in greater detail, taking us a step closer to seeing things as they really are.

Thus, whatever we do, if we have total concentration and mindfulness, we can transform an ordinary experience into an extraordinary one, a worldly experience into a spiritual one, and ordinary vision into insight.

"Better it is to live one day wise and meditative than to live a hundred years foolish and uncontrolled."[16]

—The Buddha

Chapter 2
The Preparation

Now that we have looked at the many benefits of meditation, we can get down to the actual practice! We will start with the physical and mental preparation for meditation.

The sitting postures are important because we need to keep the body stilled for the mind to focus. Thus, choose one that allows you to be still for as long as possible. No one posture is best. It is all down to personal preference. You will only know by trial and error. The following guidelines will give you some ideas to what has worked the best for most people. Experiment with it.

2.1 Postures in Meditation

Wear loose, comfortable clothing and sit in any way that allows to you sit *still* with a straight back for a long time without leaning against anything. For most people, this means sitting cross-legged on the floor with a cushion supporting your bottom. But if you find that uncomfortable, you can also sit on a chair. However, once you are used to sitting cross-legged, you will find that more stable and less fidgety than sitting on a chair, so it is worth a try.

It is important to choose a comfortable posture (but not so comfortable that you'd fall asleep) because pain arising from sitting can interfere with your meditation, and your focus will be shifted to the pain rather than the meditation object. You should just need a very slight effort to maintain the posture, and your body should not be too stiff, slouching, or leaning backward.

The postures I have found most comfortable are:

1. The Burmese or "comfortable" posture

Sitting on the floor with a cushion supporting your bottom and the legs folded inward, both legs resting on the floor, one in front of the other. This posture is very stable and comfortable, and there is no pressure on either of the legs. If you sit many sessions a day, you can alternate which foot goes on the outside.

2. The quarter and half lotus postures

This technique is similar to the above but with one leg resting *on* another. This posture is comfortable enough for up to one hour of sitting; after that you might feel some pressure and pain on the leg being rested on and also on the knee of the resting leg.

In the quarter-lotus position, your foot rests on the calf of the other leg. In the half-lotus posture, your foot rests on the inner thigh of the other leg.

3. The full lotus

This posture involves putting both feet over the other leg. It is a very stable posture if you can get used to it, but if not, it can be uncomfortable because there is pressure on the knees, ankles, and calves.

4. Sitting on the edge of a chair

Sit toward the edge of a chair. Keep your back straight and do not lean on the backrest. Put your feet flat on the floor, a few inches apart. The thighs should be nearly horizontal. You might need a cushion underneath the feet if your legs are too short.

5. Kneeling

This involves kneeling with both feet pointing backward. You need a cushion supporting your bottom, or you can sit on a meditation stool.

It is useful to be familiar with a few different postures so that if you are sitting for a long time, such as during a retreat, you can alternate between different positions to avoid pressure on the same areas. Even if you use the same posture, it helps to reduce tension on the knees by swapping the legs between different sessions.

A few things to note about the body parts:

The Head, Face, Eyes, and Mouth

- The face, eyebrows, cheeks, and jaw should be relaxed.

- The mouth should be closed, with the tip of the tongue touching the gum line of the upper teeth. This helps to reduce saliva production. Breathing is entirely through the nose during meditation.
- The eyes should be gently closed.
- Avoid squeezing the eyes and frowning.
- The chin should be slightly tucked in.

Shoulders, Arms, and Hands

- Shoulders should be relaxed and slope downward.
- Do not hunch your shoulders.
- Arms should be hanging loosely with the hands either cupping the knees, resting in the lap, or hanging over the shins.
- There should be slight, but not extra effort required keeping them in position.

The Back

- Imagine a string from the ceiling is holding you up by the crown of your head.
- The spine should be upright, with a slight natural inward curve above the waist.
- The back should be straight but relaxed, not stiff or tense.

Things to Check

- Do you feel balanced, comfortable, and relaxed?
- Try rocking your body slightly back and forth and side to side. You will find a position where the body feels naturally centered and stable.

- When you relax, are you slumping? Slumping can cause dullness and drowsiness.
- Are you tilting backward (over-arching)?
- Make sure you are not holding yourself too stiffly.
- Is your back relatively upright (with a slight inward curve)?
- After some time, your posture may slump. You can straighten up slightly, but do it very slowly and gently to avoid disturbing your meditation.
- In the beginning, it may be useful to get someone to correct your posture, or you can check yourself in the mirror.
- Before you start, scan the body from head to toes to ensure all the muscles are relaxed, and gently release any tension you found along the way.
- When you finish, avoid getting up quickly. Be mindful when you open your eyes. Move slowly and mindfully.

I should mention here that although some traditions employ the *mudra* (certain finger and hand configurations) during mediation, I myself have never used it, nor have I witnessed any of Theravadan monks using it. By all means use it if it makes you feel at ease, but just make sure you are not paying too much attention to keeping such a position, since it might distract you from the meditation object.

Although I have listed many details above, do not become overly obsessed about it. You may find you'll only need to check the entire list once or twice, and after that you can quickly get into the posture you feel comfortable with. There is no need to go through the whole list every time. The important thing to remember is just to keep still with your back straight.

2.2 The Preliminary Practice

Once you are in a comfortable posture, you can prepare the mind for concentration. Begin every meditation with this preliminary stage to settle your mind in the present moment and to set determination for concentration.

I. Sit in a comfortable posture.

II. Tell your mind to be alert, attentive, and stay in the present moment. Let go of all the mundane stuff — at least for the duration of this sitting. View *all* thoughts (no matter how important they seem) as distractions during the course of the meditation. You have plenty of time to deal with them after the meditation. Any attempts to get involved in ideas or notions, no matter how important they seem, are just tricks of the mind.

III. Center yourself in the present moment: be aware of where you are, the sounds you can hear right now, feeling your weight on the cushion, the feeling of clothes and air brushing against your skin. Be aware of all that you can hear and feel *externally*.

III. Scan your body from head to toes, as if water is pouring from the top of your head. Be aware of each part of the body and letting go of any tension you found along the way: the scalp, face, neck, shoulders, arms, hands, trunk, buttocks, thighs, calves, and feet.

IV. Now turn your attention inward and focus on the inner silence. That is the *space* between thoughts. Notice how peaceful that feels. Relish it.

If you find it hard to observe the space between thoughts, you can try holding your breath for just one to two seconds — don't hold it for longer, though (and there is no need to keep repeating this).

Spend a maximum of five minutes on the entire session. After one to two weeks, you should be able to quickly scan the entire body in less than one minute.

A beginner should repeat step IV several times per session.

It is also useful to do step IV when you are lying in bed, because it helps to relax your body, making it easier to fall asleep.

Chapter 3
Metta
(Loving-Kindness) Meditation

Metta is a practice that develops concentration and cultivates altruistic love, goodwill, and friendliness toward oneself and others by supplanting hatred, ill will, and hostility.

In countering ill will, which is a major hindrance to meditation, *Metta* calms the mind, allowing it to settle into a deeper meditative state. Not only is *Metta* a powerful calm practice on its own, but since it suppresses the hindrances, it also reinforces all other types of meditation.

Practicing *Metta* is also a way of getting in touch with our true nature, since our radiant mind is imbued with loving-kindness and wisdom (as explained earlier).

To some, it might sound contrived to "cultivate" feelings of love and goodwill, but the fact is we are generating feelings all the time. But often we create anger, resentment, and jealousy instead.

Since the mind is a compound of constantly changing mental conditions, we can skillfully nurture the positive ones for the mind, instead of letting it do what it will. It is like tending a beautiful garden instead of letting it grow wild.

This meditation is easy to do because your focus is not tied to a single object; it is also less restrictive, since we allow imagination to roam.

Metta practice leaves you with a positive and uplifting spirit, making it an ideal antidote for depression, restlessness, anxiety, and sleeping disorders. You should always turn to this practice if you find you are struggling too much with Mindfulness of Breathing meditation.

How to Practice *Metta*

Metta practice is done in stages. First, we send *Metta* (loving-kindness) to ourselves, because if we don't feel good about ourselves, we are not likely to be generous and kind to others. Then we send *Metta* to a person we admire and respect (normally we avoid using someone who might arouse lust).

Next, we move on to a "neutral person" (someone we feel impartial about). After that, we send *Metta* to a hostile person, but we only do this after we have generated a sufficiently strong feeling of *Metta*.

The next stage is dissolving our selfish biases in "breaking the barriers." And finally, we extend *Metta* to all sentient beings.

Please note that if you can't find anyone you love and respect, you can also send *Metta* to an animal or even a plant. The point is, choose an object that easily arouses warm, altruistic love, and then build on it. It's just like when lighting a campfire: you start with the most combustible items such as dried leaves and twigs before putting on larger pieces of wood. Once the fire is strong, you can throw in the sappy logs. In a raging fire, even metal melts. You start with an object that easily evokes your love and compassion. Once your altruistic love becomes strong, you can even be compassionate toward your enemy.

You can vary how you do *Metta* to suit, as long as it generates a *genuine* positive emotion. Below is a step-by-step instruction for doing *Metta*.

1. *Metta* Toward Yourself

After the Preliminary, focus your attention on the center of your heart.

Note your current mood and emotion. Then cultivate loving-kindness for yourself with the affirmation:

May I be well…
May I be happy…
May I be free from suffering…

As you verbalize the affirmations, see what your mind conjures up (pictures, scenes, notions) and feel the effect it has on your emotion. Capture that emotion and amplify it by repeating the affirmation and using visualization.

For example, when you say, "May I be well," you might imagine pure universal energy in the form of white light flowing into your body through the crown of your head. See the energizing light spreading throughout your body. Generate a sense of well-being and rejuvenation with this visualization. Feel yourself getting stronger, fitter, and more energetic. Or you might visualize a light inside your body below the navel that gets bigger and brighter.

As you repeatedly run through the visualization, your emotion should intensify.

Some people prefer visualizing a sun (which represents love) in the center of their heart. As they do the affirmation, they visualize it expanding and getting more intense.

Another way is to recall the time when you were the strongest and fittest; perhaps you were doing the sport that you enjoyed. Bring yourself back to that moment. How did that feel? Perhaps you felt invincible then? Build on that emotion by replaying the scene several times or from different perspectives.

Use whatever visualization or imagination you can to generate a *genuine* emotional response.

Similarly, when you verbalize, "May I be happy," visualize a time when you were the happiest. Perhaps you had just passed your exams, or were on holiday, or were doing something else that you enjoyed. Relive that experience and amplify that positive emotion.

When you say, "May I be free from suffering," you might think of all the positive things that are going on in your life. Realize how fortunate you are to be having the things you have today — things could always be worse. For example, I'd be grateful for my health. I am happy that I am not suffering from any illnesses right now. Because when you're ill, no matter where you are or what you have, you'll still feel miserable. We often take our health for granted — until we become ill.

There are many things that could make my life worse than what I have right now, so I am grateful they are not present. Appreciate all the things you have, and that will make you feel great about yourself.

You can do one affirmation at a time, or you can verbalize all three affirmations repeatedly and see what your mind conjures up. You are only limited by your own imagination with this exercise.

2. *Metta* for a Person You Respect

Think of someone you admire and respect. Or you can also think of your parents. And repeat the affirmations:
May he (or she) be well...
May he (or she) be happy...
May he (or she) be free from suffering...

Perhaps you can visualize them doing what they enjoy. You can also recall a time when you saw them the healthiest and happiest. See their smiling face in your mind's eye. Have a genuine want for them to be happy and see how that makes *you* feel. And then build upon this feeling.

3. *Metta* for a Neutral Person

By now, your *Metta* should be getting stronger, so you can extend it to someone you normally feel neutral about (neither like nor dislike). This person might be an acquaintance such as the postman. Apply the same affirmation:
May he (or she) be well...
May he (or she) be happy...
May he (or she) be free from suffering...

Have a genuine wish for this person to be well and happy. How does it make *you* feel?

4. *Metta* for a Hostile Person

You can even extend *Metta* to someone you don't normally like or get along with. But you can only do this when your *Metta* is strong. It's like a raging bushfire that can consume anything in its path — dried wood, sappy wood, and even metal. Your *Metta* is now so strong that even a hostile person does not dampen it. Repeat these affirmations:

May he (or she) be well...
May he (or she) be happy...
May he (or she) be free from suffering...

Remember, you don't have to *like* this person, but you can still feel compassionate love for them.

One good reason to wish them well would be if they were happier, it would make everyone's life easier! And if everyone is happy, the world is a much better place.

Since everyone is different, it is okay if you don't get along with him or her. However, they are just as entitled to their happiness as everyone else.

If you find this stage difficult to do, just leave it out until your *Metta* is strong enough to practice it. You will know when you are ready to try again.

5. Breaking the Barriers

This takes it a step further. Your *Metta* is now so strong that you see no one's welfare as more important than others. At this stage, you do not wish that you were better off than anyone else, and you have no bias toward your friend over a hostile person. You genuinely wish everyone could enjoy an *equal* amount of happiness and well-being.

In this meditation, imagine you, the person you respect, the neutral person, and the hostile person are all enjoying equal amount of prosperity.

Use these affirmations:
May we be well...
May we be happy...
May we be free from suffering...

You might visualize all of you sitting in a circle or at a table, sharing *equal* amounts of prosperity and well-being. For example, if there is a prize given to one of you, be equally as happy for whoever receives it.

6. Extending Your *Metta*

The next stage is extending *Metta* to all sentient beings. Starting from where you are, you affirm:
May all beings be well...
May all beings be happy...
May all beings be free from suffering...

Radiate *Metta* to all the beings in your house, then expand to your neighborhood, the town, district, country, the world, and beyond this planet to encompass the entire universe. Perhaps you can visualize this as an expanding white light encompassing the entire universe.

Include all beings, in all directions, human and non-human, near and far, seen and unseen — reflect what that feels like emotionally. Hold on to that feeling for a few moments and then imagine putting all that into your heart. The love for all beings is now stored in your heart.

About the Stages

You might spend about five minutes at each stage. At the beginning, or when you have little time, you can just do stages 1, 2, and 6.

I found spending about five to ten minutes on stages 1, 2, and 6 prior to doing other meditations helps to settle the mind much quicker.

Chapter 4
Mindfulness of Breathing
(*Anapanasati*) Meditation

Mindfulness of Breathing is the main practice for developing concentration and mindfulness by focusing the attention on a single object.

It is obvious to anyone who meditates that the mind is always looking for something to latch on to: reminiscing about or regretting about the past, fantasizing or worrying about the future, plus the constant commentary and chat going on in the background, whether you like it or not. In fact, you may find it shocking the first time you discover this. Yet this is the madness you have been living with all your life! And the only time you'll experience real peace is the day you manage to quell all the noise in your head. Then, suddenly, everything will seem so quiet! It is as if you have gone high up the mountain, and now that you're enjoying the serenity, you are realizing just how chaotic it was before. This is what mindfulness of breathing can to do your mind. It calms the mind by weakening the "hindrances" and brings about a refined level of focus, alertness, concentration, and serenity beyond the ordinary state.

However, when you first start to meditate, the simple act of paying attention to the breath becomes extremely challenging. You will be surprised at how poor your concentration is; you can barely stay attentive for even a second! Don't worry, it's not just you — it's the same for everyone. In fact, some beginners just find it impossible to just focus on the breath, so they soon give up. This is because they jump straight into the deep end. What did I mean by that? Well, as mentioned earlier, your mind is normally full of thoughts and commentary, so you can't expect to just suddenly switch everything off and concentrate solely on the breath. Thus, it is virtually impossible for most beginners to detect the subtle sensations of breathing. You would need to calm the mind down gradually, and to do that you'd have to do it *systematically* to achieve total mindfulness of breathing. Only then will you be able to pick up the subtle sensations of breathing.

Thus, what follows is a systematic way to train mindfulness of breathing. It has four stages prior to the full, sustained attention on the breath. This gradual approach turns a seemingly impossible task into achievable outcome even for a complete beginner. However, you may still find it difficult to start with, but like anything else, practice makes perfect, and consistency and effort are the keys to success.

After some period of practice, you will get to a stage where all of a sudden it becomes much easier to focus, your mind "sticks" to the object of meditation, and you won't need to apply as much effort. You will then enjoy the meditation much more, and you won't feel physically tired and stiff after the sitting. You will also be able to detect the subtle sensations of breathing even as you walk in windy conditions. This period is usually at the point where you start to experience the *nimitta*,[17] which is a vision, such as a light or an object, in your mind's eye. However, for now, just take one step at a time, and do *not* long for the *nimitta* when you sit.

It is very important that you understand the method clearly before you begin, otherwise you may start to ponder or have doubt, which will ruin your practice.

4.1 Stage 1: Mindfulness with Labeling

You should begin the meditation with the Preliminary stage as described earlier and then direct your mind on the breath. This is how you do it:

How to observe the breath

Narrow your focus to the areas of the upper lip and the entrances of the nostrils. As the natural breath goes in and out, you will feel the *sensation* of air somewhere in that area. Note the spot where you felt the sensation and just focus your attention *there* and observe the breath as it passes over *that* area. Do not move your attention to other areas. Please note that breathing is entirely through the nose, so keep your mouth closed.

Just as a gatekeeper is alert and mindful of anyone passing the gate, you have to try to be mindful of every breath passing over this spot. Also, a gatekeeper only notices who goes in and out of the gate and does not follow them; you are paying attention to the breath at one location and not following it in or out beyond that spot. One of my teachers used to tell me I should observe the breath the way someone saws a piece of wood — one doesn't look at the saw or the wood, but rather the point of *contact* between the two. In the same way, when you observe the breath, you should not only focus on the breath or the area of the upper lip, but also on the *contact* the breath makes with the skin on the upper lip.

In the beginning, you may not feel the touch sensation of the breath on your upper lip area. It does not matter. You must wait patiently at this spot until you can feel it. If you cannot feel the physical sensation of the breath, do not try to create it (such as by forcing the breath or imagining it) or searching around for it. And you must *not* control or interfere with the breath in any way. You are just paying attention to the *natural* breath, that's all. It does not matter if the breath is long or short, shallow or deep, fine or course — do not try to change it. You have to observe the breath as it is. In this way you are observing reality, moment by moment.

Observe the breath as if you are a scientist observing an experiment, in a relaxed and detached manner. It helps if you do not identify it as "my breath" but instead regard it as a natural phenomenon. Feel the breath as if you are feeling it for the first time. You have been breathing every moment of your life, but have you ever observed it closely? You will be surprised what you'll discover about the breath.

Pay close attention to the breath, without turning away, going to a blank space, thinking, or imagining.

Notice when your attention has wandered off to other things, and just gently bring it back to the breath, noticing any annoyances that may arise in the mind and letting go of them. Try not to get involved in trains of thought. Stay intent on directing your attention back to the breath as soon as your mind starts to wander, since it will be much harder to get back to the breath if you start indulging in thoughts. Your mind will try to trick you into thinking, so it's best to try to pay no heed whatsoever to *any* thoughts that arise in your mind during your meditation. View *all* thoughts as distractions, and it is useful to tell yourself that before you even begin the meditation.

However, no matter how hard you try, you will be distracted by thoughts at some stage. When this happens, do not feel frustrated or discouraged. The fact that you recognized it at all is a good indication of your mindfulness. Be patient with yourself, and be open and accepting of your distractions, knowing that with continued practice, your mind will wander less. Being frustrated will only make it worse — all types of aversion are forms of "hindrances" (obstacles) in meditation. This way, you are training not only your mindfulness and concentration, but you are also developing your patience and acceptance of the way things are. The last attribute is also an important component for insight meditation.

The Labeling

If you're new to meditation, you might find your mind gets distracted very easily, that it is hard to stay focused on the breath for more than even a second. Thus, at this stage we use labeling to bolster your weak mindfulness to help you remain focused on the breath. This is rather like using a walking stick for support when your legs are unsteady. This is done by mentally verbalizing the word "out" at the *end* of each out-breath. Do not say it out loud — say it only in your head. You do not need to label the in-breath. You can of course substitute another word if you like, but keep it short, to a maximum of three syllables. Sometimes I use "concentrate"; in that case, at the end of every out breath I would mentally note, "concentrate." This is really useful if your mind is too distracted to focus silently on the breath. You can also use this when you are walking. It's a great way to keep your mind from running on.

4.2 Stage 2: Mindfulness with Counting

The Counting

This counting stage is a step further in strengthening your mindfulness, and it requires slightly more effort and concentration.

This is how it's done: count "one" at the *end* of the first out-breath, and then "two" at the end of the second out-breath, and so on, up to a count of *eight*. Eight counts makes up one "set." Just count in your head, not out loud. The reason why we don't count to ten is because you have to apply more mindfulness counting to eight than ten, which is habitual for most people. But you are also free to choose a set of five to ten counts if you prefer. For the sake of explanation, I'll stick to a set of eight counts for now. By the way, if you find you are even struggling with a set of five counts, then you should just go back to doing Labeling or *Metta* until your concentration is better.

During counting, if you have wandering thoughts, you have to reset the counting to start from one.

Thus, a set of eight counts has to be a "clean" set — with no distracting thoughts. For example, when you have counted to seven and started to have wandering thoughts, you must go back to counting from one again. If you found yourself counting up to ten, then you have lost mindfulness (because we are only supposed to be counting up to eight), and so you would have to go back to counting from one (and thus having to repeat that set).

Insisting on a "clean" set of eight counts help to strengthen the resolve, focus, and mindfulness. I found this develops mindfulness in a number of ways: you have to remember to count after each breath, you have to know whether it's an in- or out-breath as you are only counting at the end of the out breath, you have to remember that one set is eight counts, and you have to be aware of whether you have invading thoughts. Since you are so busy doing so many tasks, you won't have time to think! This is how you trick the mind into letting go of thoughts. As my teacher said, if you are concentrating properly on the breath, it would not be possible to think. If you are thinking, then you are not concentrating properly — you are not doing your "job"!

I also found counting to be a good way to measure your progress in mindfulness, since you will not have to repeat the set as frequently when your concentration improves.

You can set yourself a goal to be able to do a certain number of sets without repeating, and then to increase the number of sets with each subsequent meditation session. For further details, see the end chapter on Systematic Progressing.

This counting method made a huge difference in my practice. Without the counting, when your mindfulness is not strong, you might find yourself indulging in all kinds of daydreams without even realizing it. So if you were doing silent Mindfulness of Breathing and found you became distracted easily and often, then revert to this counting method, and it will keep a tighter rein on your mind.

4.3 Stage 3: Long or Short

To develop your power of concentration and mindfulness further, you need to pay more attention to the breath by identifying its attributes, such as noticing whether the breath is long or short.

This exercise requires more mindfulness and longer concentration because you have to observe the entire breath length to know whether it is a long or a short one.

You probably realize by now that we are increasing the "difficulty" level incrementally with each stage, until you can do Mindfulness of Breathing silently and properly, without feeling like you got thrown into the deep end.

So, at this stage, you observe the breath for a minute or two to arbitrarily decide what is the "average" length of the breath so that you can gauge whether the present breath (that is about to finish) is long or short relative to that.

Your attention is still staying at the spot where you feel the sensation of the breath going in and out of the nostrils.

When noting, it is just *knowing*, rather than verbalizing "long" or "short," although you can say "long" or "short" in your head a couple of times at the start if you find it helpful. But if you keep verbalizing, your mindfulness will be applied more to the verbalization than to the breath itself.

4.4 Stage 4: Beginning, Middle, or End

This is a variation of the one above. I found it useful to alternate between the two to keep the mind fresh and alert.

In this exercise, you need to know whether the *section* of the breath you are experiencing right now is the beginning, middle, or the end of the breath cycle. And the only way to know this is to be mindful of the *entire* breath cycle, thus forcing yourself to be more attentive.

As above, with regards to the noting, there is no need to verbalize "beginning," "middle," and "end," although you can do this a couple of times at the start if you like.

4.5 Stage 5: Full, Sustained Attention on the Breath

At this stage, unlike previously, you are required to pay attention to the *entire* length of the breath, from the beginning to the end, not just parts of it. And you are not using any of the supporting "tools," so no labeling, counting, or noting of any sort, just pure awareness of the breath at the point of contact with the upper lip. Remember the saw metaphor I mentioned earlier.

Observe the breath as it moves smoothly through its cycle and then turning around to start a new one. I found it helpful to apply a little extra mindfulness in observing the end of the cycle, because it is very subtle, and, without that extra mindfulness and concentration, you can easily miss it.

This is the highest *samadhi*[18] stage so far. At this stage, your mind happily remains focused on the breath, and you will find that you do not need as much effort to fixate on it. You will enjoy the meditation, and you can sit for longer without feeling soreness or stiffness; even noise will not bother you as much. If, however, none of these descriptions apply to you, then you probably have moved on to this stage too soon, and you had better go back to the previous stages.

Summary of the Stages:

Stage 1: Focus on the area of the upper lip and the entrances of the nostrils, stay at the spot where you feel the sensation of the breath, and label "out" at the end of each out-breath.

Stage 2: Focus on the area of the upper lip and the entrances of the nostrils, stay at the spot where you feel the sensation of the breath and count from one to eight, each at the end of the out-breath.

Stage 3: Stay at the spot where you feel the sensation of breath and notice if the present breath is long or short.

Stage 4: Stay at the spot where you feel the sensation of breath and notice if the present section of the breath is the beginning, middle, or the end of the breath cycle.

Stage 5: Stay at the spot where you feel the sensation of breath and observe the entire breath cycle continuously, paying extra attention at the turns.

Working With the Stages

I would advise you to build up a good foundation at each stage before moving on to the next. Do not be in a rush to try the "higher" stages. If the foundation is not strong, your meditation will regress if you move on too early. It is better to stay too long at one stage than to move too quickly to the next stage.

Once you have reached the higher stages, any time you feel your mindfulness and concentration insufficient to perform, just move back down to the lower stage(s). For example, if you find you cannot even count up to eight (during stage 2) without having to repeat the set many times, then you should go back to Labeling or do *Metta* practice instead of carrying on struggling with counting. If you find you struggle with Labeling, then go back to *Metta*. In this case, you keep doing *Metta* until your concentration is good enough to do Labeling, and you will know when you've reached that point.

Even within the same sitting, you can move up and down the stages depending on how good (or not) your concentration is. You must be flexible and work with your present mental condition. If you are bored with Mindfulness of Breathing or have a very discursive mind, go back to *Metta*. Often, you might have some anxiety or stress that prevents you from concentrating on the breath, so when you revert to *Metta*, it fixes this problem (often you don't realize there was stress or anxiety there until you feel a difference after you have done *Metta*).

On the other hand, if your concentration is good enough, you can go straight to stage 5 after the Preliminary (without having to go through stages 1 to 4). The key here is to be flexible and work with your *present* mental condition, just as a skilled craftsperson knows what tools to use and when to use it. This is the systematic way to do meditation.

4.6 Concentration *(Samatha[19])* Walking Meditation

The benefits of walking meditation are:

- It enables one to maintain continuous meditation practice throughout the day (when not doing sitting meditation).
- It provides the benefits of exercise.
- It relieves soreness and stiffness from sitting.
- It overcomes sloth and torpor.
- A change of environment helps to freshen and brighten the mind.

- Some meditators can only do walking meditation since they find it difficult to sit for long periods of time.
- It is a good way to integrate meditation into normal daily activity.

How to Practice Walking Meditation

This way of doing walking meditation is what I call concentration (*samatha*) walking meditation. It is an extension of the sitting Mindfulness of Breathing meditation. Here, you carry on the same practice as the sitting one but in a walking mode. This is useful for alternating with sitting sessions to avoid stiffness and soreness and to fight off drowsiness. This is how to do it:

- Walk in a normal, relaxed manner — you do not have to do it in slow motion (the way some people would with "insight" walking meditation).
- Direct your gaze to about five meters in front. You are just looking to make sure you don't walk into things, so don't look around admiring the scenery! You must remain blinkered and in your own world so that you can concentrate on the meditation object.
- You should focus your concentration on only *one* spot, the area above the upper lip where the sensation of the breath is normally felt. Even when you cannot feel any sensations there, you should, nevertheless, concentrate on *just* that location and not become distracted by anything else.
- When lost in thought, you can stop walking for a few seconds, since that helps to break the train

of thoughts. Center yourself again with awareness of the location of the upper lip.
- I found it useful to play a "game" while I am doing this exercise. I would try to go from point A to B without having distracting thoughts and then try to extend it further each time. You can experience incredible tranquility if you can go a long way without being interrupted by thoughts.

4.7 The Sound of Silence Meditation

Begin with the Preliminary stage, then turn your attention inward and focus on the inner silence. That is the *space* between the thoughts. Notice how peaceful that feels. It is here that you'll find the "sound of silence, " a tinnitus-like humming sound that is almost like electricity in nature. If you concentrate on this sound, it will become more distinct.

I became aware of this sound years ago after I started meditating. Initially, I thought it was tinnitus, until I came across Ajahn Sumedho's book in which he called it "the sound of silence":

> *As you calm down, you can experience the sound of silence in the mind. You hear it as a kind of high-frequency sound, a ringing sound that's always there. It is just normally never noticed. Now when you begin to hear that sound of silence, it's a sign of emptiness — of silence of the mind. It's something you can always turn to. As you concentrate on it and turn to it, it can make you quite peaceful and blissful. Meditating on that, you have a way of letting the conditions of the mind cease without suppressing them with another condition.*

> *Otherwise you just end up putting one condition over another.* [20]

Staying with this sound keeps you in the present moment. The sound disappears the moment your mind turns to other thoughts. Thus, the sound of silence is your "audible feedback" tool for mindfulness.

Some people are naturally aware of this sound. For others, it takes a little bit of practice to pick up on it. But once you are aware of it, it becomes quite easy to pick up on it again. This sound is always with you, so you can tune into it at any time. All that is required is a quiet mind and a bit of concentration to set it off. Once you have the sound, it is easy to maintain.

When you focus on the sound, it becomes louder. When is it very loud, you no longer have other thoughts, since your mind is filled with this sound. I have found it a very effective way to empty the mind of thoughts.

Chapter 5
Nimitta (Visions)

When your mind is concentrated, you may see a light or an object (vision) in the mind's eye. This is called a *nimitta*, a visual by-product of a concentrated mind. This may happen with any type of meditation, but particularly so with the "calm" (*samatha*) type (such as *Metta* and Mindfulness of Breathing).

If you see a *nimitta*, ignore it. Carry on concentrating on your meditation object. If you turn your attention toward the *nimitta*, it will probably disappear. This is because the *nimitta* is the by-product of your concentration. When you let go of your meditation subject and move your attention to the *nimitta*, you are letting go of the causal condition for the *nimitta*, which explains why it disappears. It is like starting a campfire — you fan the fire to get it going, but if you keep looking at the flame and stop fanning, the flame will soon disappear, because its causal condition has been removed.

When you see the *nimitta*, try to remain equanimous. Do not be afraid of it, and also try not to get excited by it. Doing either causes it to disappear. Also, once you've seen the *nimitta*, do not keep longing for it. Do not hope or expect it to come the next time you sit, since doing so only prevents it from coming (desire is acting as a hindrance).

The *nimitta* varies depending on your consciousness. It comes as a result of the coming together of various mental conditions, so it is likely to be different at different times and in different environments. There is no need to speculate about the *nimitta*. Although you probably won't be able to help looking and analyzing it the first time you see it, because it will be the most beautiful thing you have ever seen. To describe it as astonishing and mesmerizing would be an understatement.

The *nimitta* you see may look like:

- Cotton wool
- Drawn-out cotton
- Moving air or a draught
- A bright light like the morning star
- A bright ruby or gem, or a bright pearl
- The stem of a cotton plant
- A sharpened piece of wood
- A long rope or string
- A wreath of flowers
- A puff of smoke
- A stretched-out cobweb
- A film of mist
- A lotus
- A chariot wheel
- A moon or a sun
- A bunch of roses
- A diamond
- A lick of flame (like a blowtorch flame)

I saw many more (see my book, *"Diary of a Meditator"*), and the ones you see are likely to be different. But the above lists the common ones.

When you get to a stage where you start to experience the *nimitta*, I would strongly advise you to consult an experienced teacher, since it can be an overwhelming experience. But more importantly, at this stage you can progress quite quickly if properly guided, whilst grasping and craving for the *nimitta* can lead to regression.

Suppose you are focusing on the breath and the *nimitta* arises — do *not* turn your attention away from the breath to look at the *nimitta*. The *nimitta* is there anyway, and you cannot avoid noticing it, so there is no need to "look" at it. There is nothing wrong with the *nimitta* itself, since it is just a sign that your concentration has reached a certain level, but if you start turning your attention to the *nimitta*, your concentration will drop and the *nimitta* will most likely disappear altogether. Or if your concentration is strong at the time, and the *nimitta* stays, you might be tempted to analyze and misinterpret it. Either way, it sets up expectation or fright in your mind that prevents you from getting into deep meditation later.

In the later stages, when your concentration is strong and the *nimitta* is very bright, it will not disappear even when you look at it. In fact, this is the way to the *jhana*s,[21] the deep absorption stages, but that is beyond the scope of this book.

Chapter 6
The Hindrances:
Enemies of Meditation

The Buddha said it was easier to conquer a thousand men a thousand times than to conquer your own mind.[22] Any meditator can easily relate to this.

The problem in meditation is that your enemies, more often than not, are disguised as friends. It's hard to fight an enemy you don't recognize.

Thus, the first step in overcoming the problems in meditation is to recognize the things that can prevent you from getting into deeper and calmer meditative states.

Here, the Buddha offered a solution. The five groups of mental factors that "overwhelms the mind and weaken the wisdom," he called "the hindrances" are:[23]

1. Sensual desire
2. Ill will
3. Sloth and torpor
4. Restlessness and remorse
5. Doubt

The hindrances limit and obscure the mind, making it "unwieldy" and unworkable, similar to the way gold contaminated with impurities is brittle and hard to mold into various shapes. Also, gold mixed with impurities does not shine like it should. Similarly, our radiant mind when freed of the hindrances is brilliant and shining. This is very apparent when you have attained some degree of *samadhi* — the more your mind is concentrated, the more brilliant the appearance of the *nimitta*. Prior to entering the *jhana* state, the *nimitta* often appears like an intense white light, as if you're staring at the midday sun.

As with any battle, we need to know our enemies' strengths and weaknesses in order to overcome them. Meditators should know how the hindrances arise, what makes them stronger, weaker, and how to get rid of them. This is our battle plan!

During meditation, from time to time we should examine our minds to see if any of these are present. It is easier to recognize them when you look for them, otherwise they can sneak up on you. Often, merely noticing a hindrance is enough to make it retreat.

1. Sensual Desire

This ranges from sexual desire to craving for food, comfortable lodging, and even changing to a more comfortable posture such that it causes the mind to turn away from the object of meditation toward the object of desire.

The Buddha gave metaphors for sense desire being like a debt (one has no choice but pay up — similar to the way one feels obliged toward the objects of desire), or like a dye that has colored the appearance of water so one is unable to see one's reflection in it.

The cause for their arising and gaining strength is "unwise attention" to beautiful or desirable objects.

The ways to abandon them are:[24]

- Meditate on impure objects (seeing the foul aspects of those desirable objects).
- Guarding the sense door (be careful what you pay attention to lest greed for a desirable object or aversion to an undesirable object arises).
- Moderation in eating (heeding greed for food).
- Noble friendship (mix with respectable people who can set a good example).
- Suitable conversation (not engaging in talk that disturbs the mind and loses the focus of the meditation object).

2. Ill Will

This can be any form of aversion, from hatred to anger to mild irritation or annoyance. This can be toward other people or oneself, such as having difficulty with your meditation and not liking it.

The metaphor for ill will is having an illness, which makes everything sour and bitter; the world is a bitter place for someone who possesses ill-will. Another metaphor is having a mind like boiling water that prevents one from seeing one's reflection; ill will distorts the view of the world.

The cause of their arising and gaining strength is also "unwise attention" to them.

The ways to abandon them are:

- Meditate on loving-kindness (*Metta*), compassion, sympathetic joy, and equanimity.
- Consider that everyone is subject to their karma (there is no need to plan revenge on someone who has done you wrong).
- Consider that anger is like picking up hot coal to throw at someone (you will burn yourself first).

- Noble friendship — as above (1.)
- Suitable conversation — as above (1.)

3. Sloth and Torpor

This is physical and mental lethargy: laziness, dullness, sluggishness, drowsiness, and sleepiness. The mind goes into a blank space instead of focusing on the task in hand.

The metaphor for sloth and torpor is water covered with moss and weeds, where one cannot see one's reflection.

The cause, again, is "unwise attention" to them.

The ways to abandon them are:

- Exertion (putting more effort into it)
- Pull your ears
- Wash your eyes
- Walk up and down
- Change posture
- Thinking of the perception of light (imagining a bright light makes you feel more alert)
- Stay outdoors
- Avoid overeating (this causes sleepiness)
- Noble friendship
- Suitable conversation
- If all else fails, lie down, have a nap, and wake up fresh to meditate. I must admit this is often my number-one choice! I found a "power" nap helps a lot. It's much more productive than feeling very sleepy when you are trying to meditate.

4. Restlessness and Remorse

Restlessness is overexcitement, leading to unrest and a scattered mind. Remorse also includes worry and regret.

The metaphor for restlessness and remorse is water being stirred by wind, creating waves and ripples so that one cannot see one's own face in the reflection. Also, it is like being a slave — being chained to various emotional states.

The cause is unwise attention to them.

The ways to abandon them are:

- Knowledge of the teaching and method
- Asking questions about them
- Living a moral and ethical life
- Noble friendship
- Suitable conversation
- Developing contentedness (being happy with what you've got)
- Avoiding a fault-finding mind[25]

5. Doubt

This is skeptical doubt and vacillation: doubt about the teacher, the method, and one's own ability to perform. This causes the mind to waver and dither, unable to move forward. So one ends up doing nothing or regressing.

The metaphor for doubt is water so muddy that one cannot see one's face in it. Another metaphor is someone setting off on a journey, but upon hearing the first sound of a bird or a broken twig, they decide to turn back — fearing the bandits have come.

The cause is unwise attention to them.

The ways to abandon them are:

- Firm conviction in the teacher and method and one's own ability
- Clarification by asking questions
- Consulting with a good teacher can allay doubt in one's ability.

This covers all the potential problems you could have in your meditation. Its good to review your meditation and identify what it was that held you back from getting deeper in your meditation. Having identified the cause(s), you can find the remedy from the list above. This is the best way to identify the problems yourself if you have no access to a teacher. So now we have a clear idea who our enemies are in meditation. Be on the lookout for them![26]

Chapter 7
Insight (*Vipassana*) Meditation

Insight meditation is for "seeing things as they really are" to correct our misconception of the world, which is the root cause of our discontent.

We see impermanent things as permanent, and when they change, we suffer. We misconceive notions of the self and regard the changing phenomena such as our physical body, sensations, perceptions, thoughts, and consciousness as the self. And when they inevitably change, we suffer. For example, when we feel sad, we tend to think, "*I am* depressed," instead of thinking, "Right now, depressive emotions are being experienced, but all this *will* change (as all phenomena do, from moment to moment)."

In the first instance, not only do we wrongly identify our self with the depressed state, but it also does not provide any good prospect for the future. We have condemned our self to a kind of purgatory — that "I am" depression and depression is I! Whereas in reality all thoughts or emotions are evanescent, constantly arising and disappearing. Why should we identify our self with something so ephemeral that we often have little or no control over it? Surely if it was our "self," we should be able to control it.

With insight practice, we *deconstruct* our perception of the world that we had previously constructed based on misconceptions. We do this by observing, from moment to moment, the changing nature of the physical and mental processes (the ones we had previously assumed to be permanent). Having seen things as they really are, we can then correct our understanding of the world and our *reaction* to it. Insight practice is thus an *unconditioning* process.

Letting go of the things that cause us suffering leads to openness and freedom. We let go of craving for impermanent things when we know they ultimately bring us suffering. We let go of the attachments to "I" and "myself" when we have realized the physical and mental processes we took for "I" and "myself" were also changing phenomena.

Successful insight practice requires a high level of attention to observe the very subtle changing phenomena. Thus, a certain degree of concentration previously obtained from "calm" meditation is a prerequisite.

To understand impermanence, we need to observe change. To understand how oppressive craving and aversion are, we need to observe our attitudes toward them. We need to understand those things are impermanent and have no legitimate basis for desire or rejection.

All these can be observed within our own body: the physical postures, the breath, the sensations, the thoughts, and emotions.

The primary aim of this practice is to make you realize the key universal laws of nature for self-transformation.

1. Impermanence

Everything is in constant flux. Both mentality (mind) and physicality (matter) are constantly changing. If you carefully observe your mind, body, or any other phenomena, you would find that nothing remains the same, even for a finger snap.

We know scientifically that this is true, but we don't *feel* that way because to the naked eye things appear the same. Our normal faculties can't pick up subtle changes. Also, to some extent we are in denial about impermanence, perhaps because that makes us feel insecure. However, putting our heads in the sand only results in more suffering.

When we observe impermanence and accept it, we can learn to live in line with reality, instead of fighting against it and suffering the inevitable disappointments.

2. Craving, Aversion, and Dissatisfaction

The cause of our dissatisfaction comes either from not getting what we want or from having what we don't want. There is always an underlying psychological unrest as we face those ever-present dualities. Craving and aversion have been so deeply ingrained that they have become automatic responses, so most of the time we are unaware of them.

3. Not-Self

When we really examine our body-mind structure, we find that what we took as ourselves, our ego-center (self), is also subject to change. For example, we innately regard feelings as part of our egocentric self, but feelings are impermanent. If feelings were part of our permanent self, we would have total control of them, in which case we wouldn't ever have to suffer anxiety and depression, since no one willingly chooses to feel that way. But they are *not* subject to our direct and total control. They arise according to their causal conditions. And their disappearance is also due to conditions. These are the *not-self* aspects of feelings.

Only when you know the above principles will mindfulness be a useful tool. Therefore, *mindfulness alone is NOT enough*. So what if you are mindful of the things going around you, if your view of the world remains unchanged? Your *attitude* and *motivation* are far more important factors in self-transformation than mindfulness alone.

Another way of summarizing what I've written above is: there is dissatisfaction. Just observe it, and you'll see there is a way to end this dissatisfaction — by removing the root cause, the false views, and there is a systematic way of practice to gain insight to fix the false views that caused the dissatisfaction in the first place. What I am alluding to of course is the Buddha's Four Noble Truths: the Truth of Suffering, the Truth of the Cause of Suffering, the Truth of the End of Suffering, and the Truth of the Way (the practice) leading to the end of suffering.

Since insight meditation does not involve focusing on a single object, we can integrate it into our daily activities. There is constant change going on if we know what to look out for. Thus, there are opportunities for practice all day long.

7.1 *Vedanna*[27] (Sensation) Insight Meditation

This meditation allows us to gain the three insights discussed above from observing the physical sensations within our physical body.

1. Sit in a comfortable posture, set your resolve, and go through the Preliminary.
2. Direct your awareness to the crown of your head.
3. Notice *any* bodily physical sensations such as tingling, heat, cold, scratching, pulsing, expansion, contraction, sensations like insects crawling, or if there are no sensations at all.
4. Just be aware of the sensation (there is no need to label it).
5. Check your *attitude* toward the sensation. This is a crucial part of the meditation. You need to see what your natural gut response is to the sensation.
6. Whatever sensation you feel, be *equanimous* toward it. Do not react with craving or aversion. This step is important because it is here that you change your deep, subconscious (often unreasonable) response to the sensation. By doing this, you are rewiring your responses that otherwise would result in craving and aversion.

7. Slowly move your awareness down the body, area to area. It is best to stick to a systemic way of moving so you don't miss certain areas.
8. Stay at each area for a while. Observe the sensations and *see how they change*. See what sensations arise, check your responses to them, and apply equanimity.
9. Move slowly and systematically to cover the entire body.
10. Scan from head to toes and also in the reverse order.
11. For this practice, you need to have developed a high level of concentration (through Mindfulness of Breathing, for example), otherwise you will find your mind too scattered and will miss many subtle sensations.

The important factors to note here are:

Developing awareness of as many sensations as you can. You'll be surprised how you weren't even aware of them before and how oppressive some sensations can be.

- Observe how they change. You'll discover *all* phenomena are in constant flux. Nothing remains the same, even for an instant.
- Change your *behavior* toward these sensations by NOT automatically reacting with greed (like) and aversion (dislike). Ask yourself, "Is it reasonable to have such a response toward such sensation?"

7.2 *Citta* (Mental objects) Insight Meditation

This meditation allows us to gain the three insights discussed above by observing our thoughts and emotions.

1. Sit in a comfortable posture, set your resolve, and go through the Preliminary.
2. Direct your awareness to your thoughts; just observe them without getting involved.
3. Check your *attitude* toward the thoughts as they arise. This is a crucial part of the meditation. You need to see what your natural gut response is to the thoughts.
4. Be equanimous toward all thoughts. Do not react with craving or aversion. This step is important because it is here that you change your deep, subconscious responses. By doing this, you are rewiring your responses toward craving and aversion and not are driven by them.
5. Keep observing your thoughts as if you are watching the passing clouds in the sky. Be detached, objective, and nonreactive.

The important factors to note here are:

- Developing awareness of various thoughts and moods — see how oppressive they can be. This is what you have been putting up with all your life!
- Observe how they change. Thoughts and moods are always changing, often, without your direct control. They arise by themselves and disappear by themselves.

Change your *behavior* toward thoughts and moods by NOT reacting with like or dislike. Do not identify yourself with those changing phenomena. When observing a thought or an emotion, you should adopt the attitude: "Let me see how long this lasts." "Let me see how this will change." And then observe how it changes. Don't let yourself be the victim or a slave of a passing thought or emotion. Whatever you are thinking or feeling, it is likely to change quickly.

7.3 Insight (*Vipassana*) Walking Meditation

In this practice, mindfulness is applied to the whole body, as well as the surrounding environment. The primary aim of this practice is to make you realize the key universal laws of nature for self-transformation:

1. Impermanence

During walking meditation, observe change (impermanence). You will find it in your bodily movements, sensations, sights, sounds, touch, feelings, perceptions, and mental states. Nothing remains the same, even for a fraction of a second. Observe this objectively and with equanimity.

2. Craving, aversion, and dissatisfaction

During walking meditation, pay attention to your emotional responses to the sensory stimuli. Instead of automatically reacting with craving and aversion, act with wisdom — observe them objectively and equanimously. Resist the urge to go into automatic mode. Observe the changing phenomena and question the motivation behind those impulses. This is a crucial step for self-transformation.

3. Not-self

During walking, be mindful of the conditionality of your mental and physical structures. Try to see the underlying causes for their arising and disappearance. For example, the conditions behind moving your foot are: there is firstly an intention to lift the foot, and then the actual lifting of the foot, then shifting it, and finally, placing it down. Understand this is a process of causes and consequences. What we normally see as one movement is actually a series of movements first driven by intention (mind), followed by muscular and skeletal actions (body). These processes occur very quickly in a chain reaction, each acting as a causal condition for the next.

Similarly, when thoughts arise, try to see the conditionality for their arising. Were they set off by visual stimuli or other thoughts, or did they just arise by themselves? Were you in total control of your thoughts? Careful observation will reveal a chain of events, most of which are self-driven and autonomous, with little or no direct control from you. These are the not-self aspects.

How to Practice Insight (*Vipassana*) Walking Meditation

With the above principles in mind, let us go through this popular walking meditation technique.

- Starting from a standing still, first "center" yourself by being aware of your body, your posture, any obvious bodily sensations, the brush of the air or clothes against your skin, your mood, and emotional state.
- Walk in a slow and relaxed manner. Walk with intention and in a deliberate fashion, as if you are walking for the first time.
- Be aware of the *intention* of moving and the physical sensations as you lift each foot, moving it forward and placing it down.
- Rather than seeing it as one movement, try to see different "stages" of each movement, as if you have robotic legs or you can see the movements in slow motion.
- You may find it helpful just to observe the movements and sensations of the feet at first. Once you feel confident that you can identity many salient features involved in moving the feet, then, gradually, you can move your awareness to the rest of your body and eventually to also include the surroundings.
- Notice how you feel and how you innately respond to the things you sense. For example, if someone gets in your way, do you feel annoyance automatically arising? Do you have an instant liking or loathing of the sound of music you heard? Does the brush of cold wind instantly make you feel uneasy or withdrawn?
- What thoughts and emotions are triggered by your senses?
- Observe all phenomena objectively, as if you are a scientist observing an experiment. Be calm and equanimous. View nothing as inherently good

or bad. Avoid all judgments and biases. Adopt an attitude of curiosity toward all perceptions.
- When you found you have lost mindfulness and been carried away by thoughts, "recenter" yourself by putting all your awareness back into the feet.
- If you keep getting lost in thoughts and have walked a long way before you realized you were supposed to be meditating, then just stand still for a few seconds and reestablish the practice from the start.

Chapter 8
The Role of Wise Attention

Have you ever walked into a shop with the intention of buying one thing and then walking out with several other things, but not the one you came in for? It is easy to be tempted by the things we see and becoming sidetracked. This is an example of "unwise" attention. During a meditation retreat, unwise attention leads to distractions away from the meditation subject, our mind loses focus, and concentration falters.

Wise attention is so fundamental to meditative progress that the Buddha said, "Monks, with regard to internal factors, I don't envision any other single factor like appropriate attention as doing so much for a monk in training... A monk who attends appropriately abandons what is unskillful and develops what is skillful."[28]

Appropriate attention applies to the entire waking hours, not just during sitting meditation, and probably even more so during break times on a meditation retreat, since that's when you tend to be more off-guard. Of course, this also applies to normal daily life.

If you allow the mind to roam during these times, it can lead to hours of frustration in your sitting meditation, because unwise attention leads to unskillful mental states, like arousing greed and aversion. And once arisen, they snowball and are very hard to stop. "When a monk attends inappropriately, unarisen fermentations [defilements] arise, and arisen fermentations increase..."[29] Just like stirring up clear water, it takes a long time for mud and sediments to settle.

In *samatha* (calm) meditation, we train our attention to remain steadily on one object and not be distracted by the five hindrances. In *vipassana* (insight) meditation, our attention is trained *not* to overlook the signs of impermanence, not-self, and affliction in the objects that we normally grasp at.

The role of appropriate or wise attention is to constantly have a clear idea of the purpose of what we are doing and not letting our emotions or thoughts interfere or sidetracked us. When we are faced with unskillful mental states, there are several options:[30]

1. Observe them with equanimity. Often, this is enough to disperse them.
2. Supplant them with skillful thoughts. For example, replacing thoughts of cruelty with compassion.
3. Focusing on their disadvantages. For example, anger is like picking up hot coals to throw at someone — you'd burn yourself first.
4. Consciously ignoring them.
5. Forcefully suppressing them.
6. Reducing the energy that feeds them.

Try to see which works best for you. You may have to use a combination of ways.

Throughout the day, remain with the meditation object all day long; that way there is little opportunity for you to become distracted. And in normal daily life, find moments to be present and mindful, at least every now and then. That way when you come to sit your mind is already partly settled, and you can slip into meditation easier.

If your mind has been running like crazy for eight to ten hours before, how is it possible to experience calmness during the hour you meditate in the evening? You can't just halt the mind like that; you have to slow it down gradually. By being mindful and present every now and then, you are applying the "brake" to the mind, you are slowing it down so that when you sit your mind is already quite settled. Thus, when you feel rushed and flustered, remember to apply the brake by being mindful and concentrated. This way you are also less likely to suffer from mental overload that results in stress.

Chapter 9
Dangers in Meditation

There is nothing as beneficial and powerful as a trained mind. But like anything powerful, if mishandled, it can lead to potential harm. Below are some potential problems and dangers in meditation. If you are unsure about anything, please consult an experienced teacher.

1. Spiritual Materialism

There are all sorts of spiritual practices out there these days. In the quest for new age spirituality, some people have a tendency to amass spiritual practices and "empowerments" without critical examination. More is not always better. One of my teachers used to say, "You can dig around, but once you found something, dig deep." If you dab a little here and there, you most likely end up wasting your time. Just as when digging for water you dig a bit here and there but never dig deep enough to get any water. If you found a method that works for you, stick to that instead of chasing the next new-age fad.

Spend your time wisely; focus on practice rather than amassing intellectual knowledge through lots of reading. All the knowledge in the world isn't going to help you unless you put it into practice. It fact, that's probably going to hinder your practice because you might get confused by lots of theories. It's wisdom born of experience that can change you, not theoretical knowledge.

2. Wrong Intention

Reflect on your purpose for practicing meditation. Most people have taken up meditation for self-improvement, but some *dislike* themselves so much, they feel they need to change, and their motivation and practice is thus rooted in anger and greed, which can make things worse.

3. Dogmatic Views and Conceit

Thinking your view is the only way and denigrating others. Conceit is a hindrance, and it closes the mind to new ways.

4. Clinging to Experiences

The mind differs from moment to moment, let alone between sessions or days. If you've had blissful meditations, beware that you don't cling to those experiences and expect the same at the next sitting. Desire is a hindrance in meditation. When you sit with expectation, you are setting up obstacles. Clinging to blissful experiences stops you from progressing further. This is a very common problem amongst meditators, and people often don't even realize they are longing for past experiences. One way to tackle this is to consult with an experienced practitioner who can easily spot it from a more objective and detached standpoint.

5. Expecting Progress

This is similar to the above. It is easy to fall into this trap, so look out for it. It is hard to see it yourself but is often obvious to a teacher. Expecting progress is craving, which is a hindrance in meditation. Just do what you were supposed to do, and progress will take care of itself. Many experienced meditators will tell you that expecting progress leads to regression.

This doesn't mean you don't have an aim in your practice or that you don't need to put in effort; expectation is different. For example, I should put in effort to maintaining regular practice, and when I meditate I should make an effort to concentrate. That would be different to concentrating hard to get the blissful experience I had at the last sitting. That would be setting up obstacle right from the start.

6. Fear

Whatever visions you may encounter during meditation, just remember that is just the product of the mind at *that* time. It is best not to pay attention to the visions. For example, if you are concentrating on the breath and the visions come up, continue to focus on the breath and do not turn your attention on the visions. Don't try to analyze or interpret it. If you are not sure, consult an experienced teacher. If you are fearful, just withdraw immediately.

7. Emotionally Unbalance

If you have psychiatric, emotional, or relationship problems, it is best you attend to that first before going on a meditation retreat — and not expect meditation to transform you. If you are mentally unprepared, you may end up worse, since meditation delves deeper into your subconscious. Meditation can be used to treat depression, anxiety, and psychiatric problems, but this needs to be done gradually and systematically under strict guidance (see 1.4). Meditation is not a magic cure for psychiatric problems.

Before you go for a meditation retreat, tie up loose ends so you have no reason to think about them. Unsettled businesses will wreck havoc on your mind and likely to have an adverse effect on your meditation.

8. Trying too Hard

When you are trying too hard, you're making your mind restless and agitated, setting off the hindrances. Too much effort is also not good. Balancing effort is like tuning a musical instrument — the string cannot be too tight or too slack. A balanced effort avoids the extremes of laziness and over-exertion, which creates tension and does not allow the mind to be peaceful.

9. Repressed Feelings, Rather Than Letting Go

People often mistake letting go for repressing a feeling or an emotion. When you let go, you first acknowledge and *accept* the feeling or emotion. When you repress an emotion, you force it to go under the surface, often through denial. You probably haven't accepted it, so the problem doesn't go away. Instead, it seethes in your subconscious and later resurfaces as a bigger problem, mentally and physically.

10. The Middle Way

The Buddha struggled with austerity practice for six years before he gained enlightenment, after realizing that extreme exertion is not the way to progress. In meditation, the mind needs to be peaceful and happy to make progress. Consistent but relaxed effort along with confidence is the best approach.

Chapter 10
Putting It All Together

I have listed the benefits of meditation, and I have described in detail how to do each meditation technique. But you may wonder whether you should practice all of them, or do you pick out what appeals to you?

First of all, you must always develop concentration before insight, since without sufficient concentration you will not be able to pick up subtle physical and mental processes during insight meditation.

For a complete beginner, I suggest you start off with just the Preliminary. If even that is too hard, then do some light exercises such as yoga or Qi-Gong to develop calm and focus. If you find the Preliminary straightforward, then after a couple of sessions move on to *Metta*, which develops contentment and concentration.

Ethical Conduct

When you are practicing *Metta,* you will realize that your ethical conduct greatly affects your practice. Thus, ethical conduct forms the most basic of all requirements when it comes to the practice of meditation. Without good ethical conduct, it is virtually impossible to make progress in meditation because your troubled conscience will surface during the meditation, and you won't be able to concentrate deeply. Similarly, if you have troubled relationships, it can have adverse effects on your meditation. Therefore, it is best to clear up any misunderstandings as soon as they arise.

Basically, for deep concentration you need contentment that is dependent on a clear conscience. Hence, in the Buddha's Eightfold Noble Path, morality, which consists of Right Speech, Right Action, and Right Livelihood, forms the foundation for which concentration (Right Effort, Right Concentration, and Right Mindfulness) and wisdom (Right Understanding and Right Intention) can be developed. These eight factors support one another, such that when one or more is developed, it produces the condition for the others to be stronger. You could visualize them intertwining and leading upward in a spiral.

I would advise you to spend at least a few days on *Metta* before moving on to Mindfulness of Breathing, because *Metta* is much easier to do than Mindfulness of Breathing. But more importantly, *Metta* eliminates aversion (which is one of the hindrances to meditation), even when you don't think you are harboring aversion. In doing so it lays the groundwork for concentration to arise. For example, at one retreat center in Myanmar, it was very noisy (in fact, everywhere in Myanmar was noisy, but this one was even more so than other places), so I found it very difficult to concentrate. The neighbor's music went on all day and for most of the night, for days on end. It was like being confined in a nonstop disco. When I tried to do Mindfulness of Breathing, the thumping music reverberated in my mind. Frustrated and exasperated, I spent much time fantasizing how I could destroy the neighbors' speakers.

Eventually, I went to see my teacher, who advised that I switch to doing only *Metta*. To my surprise, after a couple of days I was able to concentrate without the music bothering me at all. And for the remaining forty days or so, I had good meditations, despite the music. I took pride in achieving this seemingly impossible task.

When I was doing *Metta*, I specifically sent loving-kindness to the perpetrators of the noise. When I could genuinely wish them well, I found my mind became calm and subdued all on its own.

Metta itself is a great meditation for developing concentration, so you can spend all your time practicing this without ever needing moving on to Mindfulness of Breathing, if you want to. Some practitioners do that — they only practice *Metta*. Once, I spent two years just practicing only *Metta*, which gave rise to good concentration and strong *nimitta*.

If you do move on to practice Mindfulness of Breathing, I would suggest you always spend at least the first few minutes on *Metta*.

When your mind is calm and contented, you can try Mindfulness of Breathing in the progressive manner that I have listed in the book, starting with Labeling. And only proceed further when you feel confident that you have successfully completed the previous step. You will be able to gauge this.

It is useful, but not critical, to have an experienced practitioner to get feedback from on your meditation in the early stages of your learning — as long as you are following the instructions carefully laid out in this book. After all, that is what this book is about! But as I said before, when you get to a stage where you experience the *nimitta*, it would be a good idea to be get personal guidance from an experienced practitioner. Although I have discussed the *nimitta* briefly earlier, everyone's experiences are different, so I think it cannot replace the role of personal guidance.

The newly acquired *nimitta* goes through "evolutionary" changes, that is, you're likely to experience different *nimitta*(s) each day or session, and this may happen over a number of days until it becomes stable and strong. At this point, your concentration is likely to be at *upacara-samadhi* (in Pali, means the "access" concentration), which is bordering the *jhana* absorption stage. The *upacara-samadhi* stage is very conducive for practicing insight, since you are now able to pick up things you could not before. So you can proceed to insight practice. Or, if you want to, you can proceed to the *jhana* absorption stage, for which you'd need to consult an experienced teacher for personal instruction. As such, I consider it beyond the scope of this book.

When I was training with the monks, we were required to have interviews (discussions about our experiences during meditation) with the teacher every day. I found their advice, especially on the *nimitta*, to be critical for my progress.

So, once your concentration is established from *Metta* and Mindfulness of Breathing practice, you can move on to practice insight meditation, as described below.

The Best Time for Practice

Most people find it best to practice first thing in the morning when their mind is fresh, and it is nice to start the day with a positive mental attitude. But that may depend on whether you are a morning or night person. You just have to experiment and see what time works best for you. If you do several sittings a day, you may want to sit longer during your most productive period of the day.

It is best to try to set a regular time for your practice; that way you can get into a routine. But practice whenever possible is the key to success. Even when you have a few minutes spare throughout the day, such as waiting in a queue, rather than getting frustrated, you can use that time to practice and enjoy the calm and peace of the present moment. So when you have a few spare minutes at work, you can focus on the breath, and when you are sitting down for a meal you can send *Metta* to those that put the food on your table. And when you are doing a task, focus on the present moment; this allows you to be more productive, objective, and less stressed. The secret is to practice as much as you can, whenever you can. A few minutes here and there adds up. If you do that, your mind is calm and not perturbed, so when you come to sit, you'll find concentration comes much sooner and easier. You can't expect to have good concentration if your mind has been chaotic all day long.

The Best Place for Practice

Try to find a private and peaceful spot at home to meditate. You can decorate it a little if you feel it can inspire your meditation. Soon you'll get into a good vibe whenever you sit there, because you have mentally associated it with meditation.

I found it useful to set a timer for the session, so that during meditation I am not wondering how long I've sat or whether I might be late for something, etc. The timer helps to discipline me to stay sitting until the alarm goes off (without it, the mind often comes up with lots of excuses why you should get up). Everything else can wait as you've already allocated this time for meditation. Be resolute. Do not get up until the alarm goes off.

Build Up Gradually

If you're a beginner, start off with just five minutes per session and then build up the sitting time gradually. Perhaps do five-minute sessions for a week and then build up to ten-minute sessions the next week, and then gradually to one-hour sessions. It would be ideal if you can do two sessions in a day, morning and evening.

Enjoy It

Enjoy your meditation, because when you enjoy it, concentration becomes much easier; see meditation as "me time." My meditation teachers always told me to "be happy" when I am not meditating, since this is vital for concentration. Remember the hindrances we talked about earlier? There is much wisdom in "be happy," since that entails you're not losing to the hindrances. If those hindrances were overpowering you, it would be hard to be happy.

Retreats

I strongly suggest you treat yourself to a meditation retreat. There are retreat centers worldwide these days, and there's bound to be at least one center or group near where you are. From my experience, it is at the retreats that you can make the significant progress. This is because you need continuous and uninterrupted concentration to push your mind to a new threshold. It is like boiling a kettle; you have to keep the heat going until it is boiled. If you keep starting and stopping, you'd never bring water to a boiling point.

You could make more progress in a ten-day retreat than in many months of one-hour sitting a day. And you can make more progress in a three-month retreat than you can in decades of one-hour sitting a day. I know this is often not practical for people, but start with a few days of retreat first. When you've experienced how beneficial it is, you will make time for it later.

Don't forget you can do a self-retreat if you cannot find a center or do not want to go to one. You just have to be self-disciplined in doing so and not get drawn into distractions. For a self-retreat, I suggest you try to follow the daily routine of a retreat center — adhere to their daily timetable and discipline. Some people make even better progress when doing self-retreats. Just make sure you understand the techniques you are practicing so doubts don't arise during your practice. If possible, arrange distant consultations with a teacher or an experienced practitioner during your self-retreat, say a thirty-minute discussion every day or every other day. It would be even better if you can call him or her whenever you need to discuss something urgently, since if you are stuck on something during a retreat, it can lead to frustration and ruin many sessions.

One of the most important things about a retreat is the mental preparation beforehand. Try to set everything in order before you enter a retreat. You just can't get into a deep meditation if you have something in the back of your mind — some unfinished business. Therefore, you wouldn't be making the most of your retreat.

A meditation retreat is not a getaway (in the sense that you are running away from responsibilities); you are there to train your mind, and you have to be in the right frame of mind to do it successfully. It should be viewed as a well-earned rest where you can indulge in some serious introspection, invoking insights that you would never get the chance to do in the midst of your daily grind.

One last thing I want to say about the retreat is that your mind gets very sensitive in deeper concentration. Beware of this and don't be reactive. It is like walking a mental tightrope at times, such that a thought or a single sentence you heard from someone might set your mind off in a chain reaction (hence the silent rule in retreat centers). If you know the mind will go into this mode, you can be better prepared. Similarly, don't indulge in reading or sending messages to someone, since you will regret having to deal with your wandering mind when you sit. Sometimes this can ruin your meditation for days. See the sections on hindrances and wise attention earlier.

Systematic Progressing

When you are able to practice Full, Sustained Attention on Mindfulness of Breathing with relative ease, you can proceed to insight meditations. It does not matter which of those you try first, but most people find Walking and Sensation insight meditations easier to do than *Citta*.

I've devised a way to help you to develop your concentration in a progressive and structured manner. I'll show you how to do this, with the help of the table below:

Prog	Prelim	Metta	Label	Count	L / S	B/M/E	Full	Insight	Total
1	2>5								2>5
2	2	5>15							7>17
3	2	20>5	5>20						27
4	2	5	20>5	5>20					32
5	2	5	5	20>5	5>20	or 5>20			42
6	2	5	5	5	20>5	or 20>5	10>30		47-52
7	2	5					30>5	15>50	52-62

10 Day Retreat
  1   All day
  2   All day
  3   All day
  4   All day/ All day
  5   All day
  6   All day
  7   All day
  8   All day
  9   All day
  10   All day

30 Day Retreat
  1   All day
  2   All day
  3   All day
  4   All day/ All day
5 to 20   All day
20 to 30   All day

Prog=Program number   L/S= Long or Short
Prelim=Preliminary   B/M/ E = Beginning, Middle or End
Metta=Metta meditation   Full = Full, Sustained
Label=Labeling   Insight=Insight meditation
Count=Counting   Total=Total in minutes

Program 1 (the first row) is a good starting point for a complete beginner. In this case, you do a daily practice of just the Preliminary, starting with just two minutes and building up to five minutes. Do this for a few days or up to a week.

In Program 2, you start off doing two minutes of the Preliminary, followed by five minutes of *Metta*. Then, each day you spend a few more minutes on *Metta* until you have reached fifteen minutes. Your total sitting time goes from seven to seventeen minutes.

Now, if you are happy just to do the *Metta* meditation, that's fine. *Metta* develops your concentration, as well as empathy and compassion, and it makes you feel good. In fact, some people only do *Metta* and nothing else.

However, if you want to develop your concentration further, especially if you want to proceed to *Vipassana* (Insight) meditation, you'll also need to do Mindfulness of Breathing, because concentration in the latter is more focused and refined than *Metta*. Furthermore, Mindfulness of Breathing produces an "internal" *nimitta* that can be used for attaining *jhana* and higher states, whereas *Metta*'s *nimitta* is "external" and cannot be used for that.

In Program 3, you start off with the Preliminary for two minutes, then do twenty minutes of *Metta*, and then you do a further five minutes of Labeling. In later sessions you gradually reduce the time on *Metta* to spend more time on Labeling, until you end up with just five minutes of *Metta* and twenty minutes on Labeling. Your total sitting time is twenty-seven minutes.

In Program 4, you start with two minutes of Preliminary, the next five minutes on *Metta*, then the next twenty minutes of Labeling and a further five minutes on Counting. In subsequent sittings, you decrease the time on Labeling whilst increasing the time on Counting by the same amount. Your total sitting time is thirty-two minutes.

In Program 5, you start with two minutes of Preliminary, five on *Metta*, the next five on Labeling, then twenty on Counting, and the last five minutes on either "Long or Short" or "Beginning, Middle, or End." It doesn't matter which of those last two techniques you choose to do since they amount to the same, but people tend to have a preference of one over another. You'll just have to see which works better for you. Again, in subsequent sittings, you decrease the time on Counting to give over to L/S or B/M/E.

In Program 6, you start with two minutes of Preliminary, five on *Metta*, the next five on Labeling, the next five on Counting, and the next twenty minutes on either "Long or Short" or "Beginning, Middle, or End" (or a combination of both), and then you do the final ten minutes on Full, Sustained Attention on the breath. Your total sitting time is forty-seven minutes. In subsequent sittings, you decrease the time on L/S or B/M/E to give over to Full, Sustained. Your maximum total time is fifty-two minutes.

In Program 7, you spend the first two minutes on Preliminary, the next five on *Metta*, then straight on to Full, Sustained Attention for thirty minutes, and then the final fifteen minutes on sitting insight meditation (you can choose Sensation or *Citta*). Your total sitting time is fifty-two minutes. In subsequent sittings, you gradually spend more time on insight and less on Full, Sustained. You can spend a maximum total time of sixty-two minutes.

By now I think you've got the idea; we are moving gradually to more difficult tasks whilst at the same time increasing the sitting time. By the time you get to Program 6, you are able to maintain full, sustained concentration on the breath for some time. If you can maintain that for thirty minutes, you are ready to do *Vipassana* (Insight) meditation, as in Program 7, where eventually you'll be spending most of your session on the insight part.

Please note, in all the sessions I always start with the Preliminary and at least a few minutes of *Metta*, since I have found these helped to settle my mind a lot quicker than if I did not use them.

The chart above also shows you how you can use this structure for a meditation retreat. Let say you are doing a ten-day retreat; you can use the first five days for developing concentration gradually, and then spend the rest of the time doing insight meditation. Similarly, on a thirty-day retreat, you would use the first twenty days for developing concentration and the rest for developing insight.

Another way to progress is to make a resolution each time you sit to have longer periods of concentration, that is, periods uninterrupted by thinking. For example, if you can maintain just one minute of concentration before any thoughts arrive, at the next sitting try to go for two minutes without thoughts. And then build up gradually but steadily.

The above programs provide you with a tangible gauge on your meditation progress. Yet another way you can tell whether you are benefitting from meditation is how much you've changed in dealing with everyday situations. Are you becoming calmer and less anxious over time? Does your anger remain as long as before? Don't expect to be a saint after some practice, but you should definitely be mellower if you're practicing correctly. If you are not progressing, check to make sure you have followed the instructions correctly and read the sections on hindrances and wise attention to identify whether one of those hindrances are stopping you from making progress.

Integrating Meditation into Daily Activities

Once your sitting meditation becomes established, try to integrate it with daily activities. You can pay attention to the breath whenever you've got a spare few minutes. Or you can use that time for insight — being aware of the present fleeting sensations, thoughts, and emotions. In both cases, you are staying in the reality of the moment, so you are therefore more alert and less stressed, since you're not weighed down by negative thoughts.

Thus, when you're out walking, make that into a walking meditation — whether it's be the concentration or the insight type. You can make gardening a meditation, cleaning a meditation, surfing a meditation, and even talking a meditation — when you are full engaged in what the other person is saying as well as being fully aware of your underlying thoughts, impulses, attitudes, and emotions.

Putting One Hundred Percent into It

Whenever you are mindful, you become more efficient and productive, you make better decisions because you are less influenced by emotions, and you enjoy the tasks at hand more. Therefore, whatever you're doing, put a hundred percent into it. So, when you're doing washing up, concentrate on the scrubbing and not on planning what you're going to have for the next meal or think about work. When are you eating, be mindful of each scoop you bring to your mouth, mindful when you are chewing, and be attentive to all the flavors in the food. Do not think about cutting the next bit of food on the plate when you still have some in your mouth.

Throughout the day, be mindful of your impulses and attitude. At the beginning, you can check periodically: "What am I thinking now?" "What is my mood?" "How do I feel?" "What is my attitude?" We have a tendency to always be a step ahead, like when we are doing something and our mind is already on to something else. When you're working, you might be thinking of eating, and when you finally sit down to eat, you're thinking about work! If you've got half your attention on your activity, you'll get half the productivity. And when the mind is always running here and there, pulling in this or that direction, stress is the result. So just slow down (remember to apply the brake), do one thing at a time, and enjoy this moment, because in less than a second it is gone forever.

You will benefit from meditation in every aspect of your life if you integrate it, so make life a meditation. Not only you will benefit personally, but you will also be able to contribute directly to society, world peace, and the welfare of all beings. After all, society is made up of individuals like yourself. If we take care of ourselves, the world will take care of it own.

I wish you success and enjoyment in discovering your mind. There is so much to explore!

Glossary

Jhana – The absorption/trance stage(s) of deep meditation
Metta – Loving-kindness meditation
Nimitta – The light/visions that appear in the mind's eye
Qi – In Chinese medicine, *qi* is energy/force
Qi-Gong – In Chinese medicine, *qi-gong* is the physical practice used to enhance internal qi.
Samadhi – A Pali word that refers to a deep, wholesome concentration
Sayadaw – "Teacher" in Burmese

Bibliography

Ajahn Brahmavamso, *Mindfulness, Bliss, and Beyond.* Wisdom Publications, 2006.

Ajahn Sumedho. *The Way It Is.* Amaravati Publications, 1991.

Harvey, Peter, *An Introduction to Buddhism: Teachings, History and Practices.* Cambridge University Press, 1990.

Venerable Pa-Auk Tawya Sayadaw, *Knowing and Seeing*, Wave Publications, KL, Malaysia, 2003.

Footnotes and References

[1] AN 1.28. *Ekadhamma Suttas: A Single Thing*. Translated from the Pali by Thanissaro Bhikkhu. https://accesstoinsight.org/tipitaka/an/an01/an01.021-040.than.html

[2] *The Dhammapada* 42-43, translated by Thanissaro Bhikkhu: https://www.accesstoinsight.org/tipitaka/kn/dhp/dhp.03.than.html

[3] My book, *Diary of a Meditator*, 2019, was based on the retreat I did with Sayadaw Venerable Eikdi Bala.

[4] You can try this for yourself. Close your eyes and see how long you can stay in the present moment.

[5] http://www.psychologytoday.com/articles/index.php?term=20010501-000025&page=1

[6] http://www.noetic.org/research/medbiblio/ch_intro1.htm

[7] http://www.noetic.org/research/medbiblio/ch_intro2.htm

[8] Ajahn Brahmavamso, *Mindfulness, Bliss and Beyond* (2006: 1)

[9] In a personal interview with the author, Quyen Ngo, in 2009.

[10] Harvey, Peter, *An Introduction to Buddhism: Teachings, History and Practices*, (2000: 245).

[11] Ajahn Brahmavamso, *Mindfulness, bliss and beyond* (2006:1)

[12] *Transcribed from a telephone interview conducted by Quyen Ngo in 2009.*

My sincere thanks to Dr. Chris Walsh, a psychiatrist working in private practice in North Carlton (Melbourne, Australia): http://www.mindfulness.org.au

[13] AN 1.49-52 [https://www.accesstoinsight.org/tipitaka/an/an01/an01.049.than.html]

[14] http://www.accesstoinsight.org/lib/thai/chah/atasteof.html

[15] MN 86. Angulimala Sutta: About Angulimala. Translated from the Pali by Thanissaro Bhikkhu. https://www.accesstoinsight.org/tipitaka/mn/mn.086.than.html

[16] https://www.accesstoinsight.org/tipitaka/kn/dhp/dhp.08.budd.html

[17] *Nimitta* in Pali means the "acquired sign," which is a mental representation of your single-focused concentration on something. It is basically a visual by-

product of a concentrated mind. You could say it is a "sign" of a concentrated mind.

[18] *Samadhi* = concentration in Pali language.

[19] *Samatha* in Pali refers to the types of meditation methods aimed at developing calm (concentration), as opposed to *Vipassana*, which aims to develop insight.

[20] Ajahn Sumedho. *The Way It Is*. The Sound Of Silence. P. 72. Amaravati Publications, 1991.

[21] *Jhana* – The absorption/trance stage(s) of meditation. In Buddhist meditation, there are the four *jhana* stages, each successive stage more sublime than the previous.

[22] The Dhammapada—Dhp VIII. *Sahassavagga: The Thousands*, translated from the Pali by Acharya Buddharakkhita.

[23] MN 10 (Satipatthana Sutta).
https://www.accesstoinsight.org/lib/authors/nyanaponika/wheel026.html

[24] https://www.accesstoinsight.org/lib/authors/nyanaponika/wheel026.html#des

[25] https://www.budsas.org/ebud/ebmed051.htm

[26] More good advice on the hindrances can be found here:
https://www.budsas.org/ebud/ebmed051.htm

[27] *Vedanna* in Pali means physical bodily sensation

[28] Itivuttaka: "This was said by the Buddha," a translation by Thanissaro Bhikkhu (Geoffrey DeGraff), Revised edition, 2013.

[29] http://www.accesstoinsight.org/canon/sutta/majjhima/mn-002-tb0.html#yoniso

[30] https://www.accesstoinsight.org/lib/authors/thanissaro/untangling.html

www.ingramcontent.com/pod-product-compliance
Lightning Source LLC
Chambersburg PA
CBHW050318010526
44107CB00055B/2299